N

MW01043211

1992

Hayit Publishing

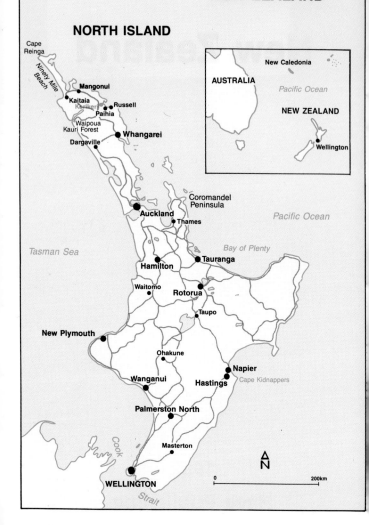

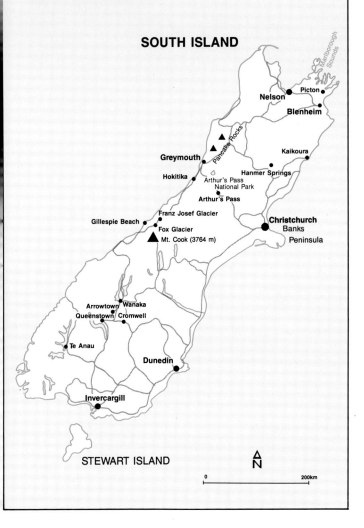

NEW ZEALAND

SOUTH ISLAND

Marlborough Sounds

Nelson • Picton •
Blenheim

Pancake Rocks

Greymouth

Kaikoura

Hokitika

Hanmer Springs

Arthur's Pass
National Park

Arthur's Pass

Gillespie Beach • Franz Josef Glacier

Fox Glacier
▲ Mt. Cook (3764 m)

Christchurch
Banks

Peninsula

Arrowtown Wanaka
Queenstown Cromwell

Te Anau

Dunedin

Invercargill

STEWART ISLAND

N

0   200km

[1st] Edition 1992
UK Edition: ISBN 1 874251 50 9
US Edition: ISBN 1 56634 008 X

© copyright 1992 UK Edition: Hayit Publishing GB, Ltd, London
    US Edition: Hayit Publishing USA, Inc., New York

© copyright 1991 original version: Hayit Verlag GmbH
    Cologne/Germany

Author: Petra Vögl
Translation, Adaption, Revision: Scott Reznik
Print: Druckhaus Cramer, Greven/Germany
Photography: Petra Vögl, Lutz Ritter

Contents

Using this Book

Books in the *Practical Travel* series offer a wealth of practical information. You will find the most important tips for your travels conveniently arranged in alphabetical order. Cross-references aid in orientation so that even entries which are not covered in depth, for instance "Holiday Apartments," lead you to the appropriate entry, in this case "Accommodation." Also thematically altered entries are also cross-referenced. For example under the heading "Medication," there appear the following references: "Medical Care," "Pharmacies," "Vaccinations."

With travel guides from the *Practical Travel* series the information is already available before you depart on your trip. Thus, you are already familiar with necessary travel documents and maps, even customs regulations. Travel within the country is made easier through comprehensive presentation of public transportation, car rentals in addition to the practical tips ranging from medical assistance to newspapers available in the country. The descriptions of cities are arranged alphabetically as well and include the most important facts about the particular city, its history and a summary of significant sights. In addition, these entries include a wealth of practical tips — from shopping, restaurants and accommodation to important local addresses. Background information does not come up short either. You will find interesting information about the people and their culture as well as the regional geography, history and current political and economic situation.

As a particular service to our readers, *Practical Travel* includes prices in hard currencies so that they might gain a more accurate impression of prices even in countries with high rates of inflation. Most prices quoted in this book have been converted to US$ and £.

Accommodation

From simple campsites to exclusive hotels, New Zealand has everything to offer.

Hotels: In the large cities, one has the choice between international hotels like the Sheraton and Southern Pacific Hotel Corporation. There are, however, also a number of private hotels, which do not always offer a high level of luxury, but are by all means up to standard.

Guest Houses: Guest houses can be found everywhere, offering simple but pleasant accommodation, often including breakfast. The concept of Bed & Breakfast hotels falls under this category and is growing in popularity in New Zealand.

Motels: Motels are another alternative for the holiday traveller, which can be found in abundance. These can, however, cost quite a lot but are appropriate for those who plan to cook for themselves because they usually offer the necessary facilities for this.

Youth Hostels: The world-wide Youth Hostel Association can also be found in New Zealand, offering accommodation for young and old alike in dormitories. These are priced between NZ$ 11 and NZ$ 15. An international youth hostel identity card is obligatory. One can also join the Youth Hostel Association in New Zealand for a membership fee of NZ$ 34.

Backpacker Hostels: Backpacker hostels are the private, entrepreneurial answer to the youth hostels. These are especially popular with those travelling on their own initiative.

Camping Sites: Whether small or large, visitors will not have to "rough it" at the camping sites in New Zealand since these are all up to the best of standards. As a rule, camping sites will be equipped with kitchens including various utensils and appliances. They are clean and often include stores and laundry facilities. The prices average around NZ$ 8; children often pay less. Campsites can often be booked as part of a tour or excursion. For those travelling with a motor home, a "power site" costs between NZ$ 15 and NZ$ 18. Most campsites are also equipped with cabins or more comfortable "tourists flats" available for as little as NZ$ 22 per person.

Information on accommodation is available at all of the NZTP offices or at other tourist information offices.

Air Travel →*Travelling to New Zealand, Travel in New Zealand*

Animals and Wildlife

The fauna of New Zealand is dominated by the sheep, but they are not indigenous to this region. At the beginning of New Zealand's history, there were no mammals at all. The island was first dominated by the innumerable birds, a few of which are still on the islands today. Many of these birds degenerated to losing the ability to fly due to the lack of natural predators. This seems to have been the case with the well known kiwi, a nocturnal bird incapable of flight. Observing this bird in the wild can only be accomplished with a lot of time, patience and a pair of binoculars equipped for night use. Even most of the New Zealanders themselves shake their heads and direct of the exhibits of the kiwi in the zoos. There, one will see a number of other flightless birds like the weka. A rarity in New Zealand is the kea, which is known as the "clown among the parrots". They live predominantly in the mountains on the South Island. One should, however, be careful. These birds have become accustomed to tourists and will grab onto anything.

The spectrum of birds, from the native pigeon to the kaka and the morepork, is extremely diverse in New Zealand. The mammals, imported by the earliest settlers, also seem to feel right at home in the "land of the great white cloud." There are no dangerous animals on the islands. In very few regions, and only with a great deal of luck, will one see the harmless tuatara lizards.

Not dangerous, but certainly annoying is the sandfly. These are small, black, biting flies which can make life quite unpleasant. They travel in swarms and live from blood. The bites can be quite uncomfortable and the itching can last for several days.

Aotearoa

The name for New Zealand in the Maori is "Aotearoa," meaning "the land of the long, white cloud." A legend recounts that a Polynesian seafarer did not first discover the island. Instead, a huge, solitary white cloud above the ocean drew his attention. One can still imagine this when observing the beautiful cloud formations, which can commonly be seen in the skies above New Zealand.

Arrowtown

Arrowtown is an old gold mining town, which has been almost perfectly restored, located only a few miles northeast of Queenstown. In Arrowtown, the past comes to life through the narrow streets and wooden and stone houses, some now occupied by souvenir shops. A short stroll through this charming village is highly recommended. With a little luck, gold can still be found in the river running through town. Those less interested in panning for gold, but who would like more information on the gold rush era can visit the *Lakes District Centennial Museum*. The museum is located on Buckingham Street, open daily from 9 am to 5 pm. Admission is NZ$ 2.50.

A truly exceptional aspect of Arrowtown is the surrounding countryside. In the region of Otago (→*Regions*), it is easy to spend hours enjoying the beauty of nature. Gently rolling hills, numerous pastures and lush green plains make this an area suited to rest and relaxation.

Arthur's Pass

The small village of Arthur's Pass is named after the mountain pass located 4 km (2½ miles) away. This is also a good starting point for car tours and hiking through the Arthur's Pass National Park (→*National Parks*).

Arthur's Pass / **Practical Information**

Accommodation: The *Sir Arthur Dudley Dobson Memorial Hostel* is located in the centre of town, offering accommodation for NZ$ 10 per person. The *Alpine Motel* is located on the main road with singles priced at NZ$ 25 and doubles at NZ$ 55.

Restaurants: Small meals and snacks are served at the *Arthur's Pass Store and Tearoom*. The *Chalet Restaurant* is less expensive.

Important Addresses: All of the necessary information is available at the "National Park Visitor Centre" in the centre of town: tips for hiking and excursions and even information on the weather.

Auckland

Auckland, the "unofficial capital" of New Zealand, has a population of 900,000, making it the largest city in the country. It was actually the capital city but lost this status to Wellington during the gold rush era. In addition to the airport, which usually serves as the point of entry and departure for most trips to New Zealand, the two harbours in Auckland are of fundamental importance. Auckland is also commonly referred to as the "Polynesian capital" because many of the islanders of the South Pacific have resettled here; this, the result of hopes for a better life from the flourishing trade and commerce. Auckland has the largest Polynesian population of any city in the world.

Geographically, Auckland is located on the Hauraki Gulf and the Tasman Sea (→*Geography*). It is home to flourishing businesses as one would expect to find in most large cities of the world. Auckland also offers a broad selection of art, cultural events and entertainment. This city is truly a good place to begin and is just as appropriate to end a visit to New Zealand. At the beginning of a visit, one can to acquire an abundance of information on the sights or to continue planning the trip in detail. At the end of a stay, Auckland offers a good atmosphere to become accustomed to the city once more after having experienced nature at its purest.

Auckland / **History**

Auckland's founding day is celebrated on September 18th, when the first governor, William Hobson, declared it the capital city of New Zealand in 1840. Before

The Keas — "the clowns among the parrots" — can most often be seen in the mountainous regions of the South Island

this, all the important responsibilities were concentrated in Russell. Prior to 1840, bloody conflicts between various Maori tribes were common. These tribes had populated the area long before the arrival of the first Europeans. For this reason, Auckland is called Tamaki (= war) in the Maori language.

During the 1860's, when the gold rush took on greater proportions, the trade centre of Wellington was declared the capital. This has remained so since then, even though many important facilities are located in Auckland. This is why the New Zealanders speak ironically about a tug-of-war between Auckland and Wellington.

Auckland / **Sights**

Finding one's way around Auckland is no easy task. The network of streets was not laid out according to any particular plan from the very beginning. To explore the city, it is best to begin with a walk down *Queen Street,* the main business and shopping street. The main post office is located directly on Queen

Auckland — the ''Polynesian capital''

Elizabeth Square. Here, there is also a bronze statue Maori warrior, which is very much worth seeing. Diagonally opposite is the Airline Terminal and a shopping centre.

Heading left from Queen Street away from the harbour, one will come upon Victoria Street West, where *Albert Park* makes a good place to relax after shopping. From here, the university campus can be seen.

The end of Queen Street is marked by the *Auckland Town Hall,* which is very much worth visiting not only because of the impressive reception rooms, but also because of the largest block of Kauri wood *(→Waipoua Kauri Forest)* in the world which stands in the foyer.

A visit to the *Auckland Zoo* is also worthwhile, where, in addition to various other animals, one will finally be able to see an authentic *→Kiwi.* Possibly even more interesting are the tuataras, the New Zealand lizards. The zoo is open daily from 9:30 am to 5 pm, admission: NZ$ 8.

Kelly Tarlton's Underwater World is located on Orakei Wharf on Tamaki Drive. The tunnel allows a view into the threatening antics of the sharks. One can get acquainted with the underwater world from 9 am to 9 pm; admission NZ$ 7.50.

A mile from the centre of the city, one can climb up the *One Tree Hill.* At the top of this volcanic cone, there was once a fortified Maori village. Today, an obelisk stands at the summit. Another observation point which can be recommended is *Mount Eden,* an extinct volcano reaching an altitude of 196 metres (641 feet).

Auckland / **Museums and Galleries**

Those with only a limited amount of time should definitely not miss the *Auckland War Memorial Museum,* located on a slight elevation in the extensive Auckland Domain park complex, the oldest city park including a botanical garden. Here, a number of Maori art and cultural exhibitions can be found as well as an abundance of general information about these Polynesian people. This museum is also educational in regard to New Zealand's flora and fauna — from current as well as pre-European times. One can also see a taxidermically prepared Moa. Now extinct, this is a flightless species of bird similar to the ostrich. Admission is free of charge; however, NZ$ 4 is charged for a "Maori tour," which is definitely worth taking. On this tour, one can form a picture of the customs and folk dances of the Maori. The war dance, "haka," is especially spectacular.

The Maori concert begins at 10:30 am and 12:45 pm. The museum is open Monday to Saturday from 10 am to 5 pm, Sundays from 11 am to 5 pm.

A collection of all types of machinery can be found in the *Museum of Transport and Technology* on Great North Road. The technically oriented will enjoy the presentation of a number of old timers. In addition, these grounds can get quite loud: during the summer, the famous rock concerts take place here. This museum is open from 9 am to 5 pm, Saturday and Sunday from 10 am to 5 pm. Admission: NZ$ 8.

Opened to the public in 1888, the *City Art Gallery* on the corner of Wellesley Street East and Kitchener Street displays the entire spectrum of New Zealand's art, documenting the country's development. It is open from 10 am to 4:30 pm, admission is free of charge.

Auckland / **Practical Information**

Accommodation: Hotels with the highest standards for those with larger budgets include: *Hyatt Hotel,* Princes St., Tel: (9) 366 12 34, NZ$ 265 per person. *Regent Hotel,* Albert St., Tel: (9) 309 88 82, NZ$ 365 per person. *Sheraton Hotel,* 83 Symonds St., Tel: (9) 79 51 32. There is also a large selection of smaller hotels and guest houses, for example: *Abby's Hotel,* on the corner of Albert and Wellesley St., Tel: (9) 303 47 99, double rooms NZ$ 83, singles NZ$ 70. *Aachen House,* 39 Marked Rd., Tel: (9) 520 23 29, doubles NZ$ 68, singles NZ$ 45. *Railton Private Hotel,* 411 Queen St., Tel: (9) 79 64 87, doubles NZ$ 66, singles NZ$ 46. *Esplanade Hotel,* Victoria Rd., Tel: (9) 45 12 91, doubles NZ$ 50, singles NZ$ 35. The *Mount Eden Youth Hostel* can be found at 5A Oaklands Road in Mount Eden, Tel: (9) 60 39 75. It is priced at NZ$ 12 per person per night. Another hostel frequented by backpack tourists is the *Georgia Hostel* at 189 Park Road, Grafton, Tel: (9) 309 95 60. A bed in the dormitories costs NZ$ 13; in a double room, NZ$ 30.

The campsites are unfortunately not very centrally located, but still can be recommended. Located about 8 km (5 miles) from the centre of the city is the *Takapuna Tourist Court* at 22 The Promenade in Takapuna, Tel: (9) 489 79 09. Spaces are priced at NZ$ 8 and there are also sites for campers or trailers. Cabins can also be rented. South of Auckland, at about the same distance from the city is the *Remuera Motor Lodge,* 16A Minto Road, Tel: (9) 574 51 26, priced from NZ$ 9.

Those who would rather not leave it up to luck, can obtain the full range of accommodation from the Tourist Information Office. These offices will usually also have information on which accommodations have vacancies.

Automobile Association: Located at the corner of Albert and Wyndham Street.

Banks: Bank of New Zealand, at the airport.

Thomas Cook Currency Exchange Office, corner of Customs Street and Queen Street (also open Saturdays from 9 am to 1 pm).

Beaches: The only beaches suitable for swimming are at the north end of the city. The seas are too rough on the western coastline.

Car Rental: A number of car rental agencies can be found at the airport. In addition there are the following: "Avis," 22 Wakefield St.; "Hertz," 154 Victoria St. West; "Greens Rent-a-Car," 89 Great South Rd.; "Buckwiser," 120 Great South Rd.

Medical Care: Auckland Hospital, Grafton Road, Tel: (9) 79 74 40 or Dr. R.W. Leitch, 11 Woodford Ave., Mount Eden, Tel: (9) 61 04 77.

Haka — the Maori war dance

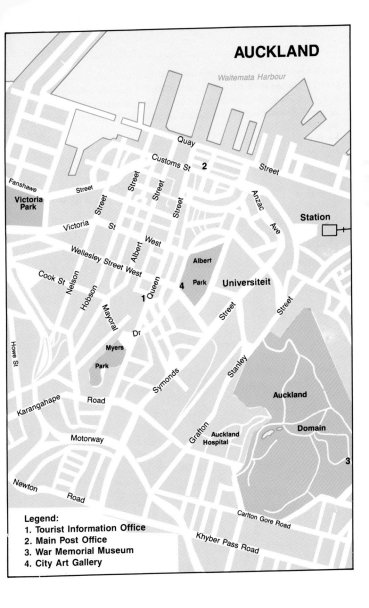

AUCKLAND

Waitemata Harbour

Quay

Customs St **2**

Street

Street

Street

Street

Street

Street

Anzac Ave

Station

Fanshawe

Victoria Park

Victoria St

West

Wellesley Street West

Albert

Albert Park

Universiteit

Cook St

Nelson

Hobson

Albert

Queen

4

1

Mayoral

Dr

Myers

Park

Symonds

Street

Stanley

Street

Howe St

Karangahape

Road

Motorway

Grafton

Auckland Hospital

Auckland

Domain

3

Newton

Road

Carlton Gore Road

Khyber Pass Road

Legend:
1. Tourist Information Office
2. Main Post Office
3. War Memorial Museum
4. City Art Gallery

Night Life: Auckland has a lot to offer with its countless pubs, in which there is often live music. In the hotels, entertainment is almost always included in the programme. *Hotel De Brett,* corner of Shortland and High St., offers entertainment every evening. This is also true for *Abby's* on the corner of Albert and Wellesley Street.

Restaurants: Auckland has something to offer for those who like the convenience of fast food as well as those with a gourmet palate, whether it is the "New Zealand Sandwich," Chinese, Indian or Vegetarian dishes — one can always find a quick and tasty meal or dine exclusively.

Among the good and reasonably priced restaurants is *Middle East,* 23A Wellesley St., for those who enjoy kebabs, salads and pitas. Italian cuisine is served in *Pisiani's,* 43 Victoria Street, and those who enjoy Mexican food will find what they are looking for at 47 High St. at the *Hard to Find Café* despite the name.

Several restaurants serve vegetarian cuisine near High and Lorne St. *Dominoes' Café,* 4 Lorne St., probably offers the largest selection of excellent vegetarian dishes. In *Simple Cottage,* 50 High St., the prices are somewhat more reasonable.

Snacks and inexpensive lighter meals are on the menu at *Peppercorns,* near the downtown bus terminal and harbour; at *Boulangerie Croix du Sud,* corner of High and Victoria St. West; and at the university cafeteria.

Pubs can be found everywhere, usually offering lunches and snacks.

Shopping: Queen Street pedestrian zone (the main shopping and business street). Simply everything can be found here.

Transportation

Air Travel: All of the larger cities in New Zealand can easily be reached from Auckland with the regional airlines. Air New Zealand has a monopoly, but Mt. Cook Airline, Ansett Airline and other smaller airlines offer flights to various cities.

Bus: A large number of the bus routes begin in Auckland and run to the larger cities or the regional points of interest. The least expensive means of transportation is the NZRRS (New Zealand Railways Road Services — the state-run bus and railway company). In addition, the public buses offer inexpensive transportation in the greater Auckland region. The bus terminal is located on Commerce Street behind the post office. From here, one can take a comprehensive tour of the city by "Explorer Bus." A bus departs for the airport every half hour; one-way fare for adults is NZ$ 8.

Ferries: The ferry departs for Davenport (Takapuna) every half hour between 7 and 9 am and from 3 to 6:30 pm; from 6:30 to 11 pm, every hour. The ferries returning from Davenport depart every half hour from 6:30 to 9:30 am and from 3:30 to 6:30 pm; from 6:30 to 11:15 pm, every hour. There are also boat excursions to the islands of Auckland departing from Queen's Wharf.

Important Addresses

NZTP — Tourist Information Office: 99 Queen Street, open Monday to Friday from 8:30 am to 5 pm, Saturdays from 9:30 am to noon.

Auckland Visitors Bureau: 299 Queen Street, open Monday to Friday from 8:30 am to 5 pm, during weekends from 9 am to 3 pm.

Police: Auckland Central Police Station, Vincent Street, Tel: (9) 79 72 40.

Post Office: Queen Street, near the harbour.

Automobile Association

The Automobile Association (AA) will serve as a guide through the entire country. This is not only true because the Automobile Association is responsible for posting all of the street signs, but also because their offices are informed about every campsite in the country. As a member of the Automobile Association, one has access to detailed route maps and excellent maps of the cities and countryside are often available free of charge. Members of the AA also have access to the efficient and speedy breakdown service and the AA tow trucks throughout the entire country. AA offices can be found in Auckland, Wellington and Christchurch (→*individual entries*) as well as in various other cities.

Banks Peninsula

The Banks Peninsula is located on the eastern coast of the South Island, offering a pleasant destination for a trip from →*Christchurch*. The two natural harbours of Lyttelton and Akaroa originated from extinct volcanoes. The geological history of this region is also apparent through the lava flows, which run over the elevations of the peninsula falling over the coastal cliffs into the ocean. Between these are idyllic coves.

Lyttelton, an important export harbour, is connected with Christchurch by a tunnel measuring 2 km (1 1/4 miles) in length. Also worth seeing is the *Timeball Station,* a building with a balloon hovering over its roof. This balloon allowed sailors to set their chronometres (open to the public).

Akaroa is the only area of New Zealand which was founded by the French. Today, it is a small fishing village.

Bargaining

Aotearoa is not the place to go if one enjoys haggling with prices. Colourful marketplaces similar to those in southern European countries are nonexistent. Bargaining with the prices of fruits and vegetables is also not possible. Numerous fruit and vegetable stands are set up along the road, but are usually not manned. One puts the money for the fresh produce in a small box at the stand. However, when the stand is occupied, it would be out of line to bargain with the already very reasonable prices.

Bay of Islands

One of the loveliest spots on earth, not only for those who enjoy sailing, is the Bay of Islands located in the northern portion of the North Island along the eastern coast. About 150 small and larger islands make up an impressive seascape. Today, these islands are no longer inhabited. Whether sailing, deep-sea fishing or simply relaxing in the sun, the Bay of Islands is definitely worth a visit.

The main centre of the Bay of Islands is a small city called Paihia, other important towns located in this area are Russell and Opua *(→individual entries)*.

Bay of Plenty

This large bay on the upper eastern coast of the North Island is separated from Hauraki Gulf by the *Coromandel Peninsula.* The bay is famous for its abundance of orchards and the excellent surfing conditions, offering something for surfers as well as spectators. It was no less than Captain James Cook who gave this bay its name: upon attempting to lay anchor, he met a hostile reception by the Maori. He then set sail and made a second attempt in the Bay of Plenty, where he was met by a peaceful reception with gifts including supplies and provisions for his crew. The most significant city in this area is →*Tauranga.* Further east is the landmark Mount Maunganui (232 metres/760 feet), with the resort town of Maunganui stretching along its base. This is a very popular holiday destination for New Zealanders *(→Maunganui).*

The Bay of Plenty has also developed into a tourist destination because of its consistently mild climatic conditions, making it a pleasant location during the entire year.

Beaches

The extreme northern part of the North Island is best known because of its →*Ninety Mile Beach,* New Zealand's most famous beach. The beach extends over 100 kilometres (64 miles). Its fine sand is so firm that it can be driven on. Another nice beach continues from Ninety Mile Beach, also along the western coast of the North Island near Dargaville.

Unique beaches can be found at the →*Bay of Islands* and →*Bay of Plenty.* Numerous smaller and more secluded coves can be found on Tasman Bay on the South Island.

A popular destination with sailors in the Bay of Islands is the "Hole in the Rock"

Blenheim

For visitors passing through, Blenheim does not hold much significance. However, this is the centre of the Nelson Region *(→Regions)* as well as being the largest city in the *→Marlborough Sounds.* Owing to the dry and predominantly sunny climate, Blenheim has developed into an important area for vineyards and orchards. Apple and kiwi plantations are concentrated in this region. The estimated 24,000 residents work mainly in this branch of the economy, with tourism taking on a secondary role.

Blenheim / **Sights**

A remnant from Blenheim's turbulent past is the old cannon from a whaling ship called *Blenkinsopp's Gun.* This historical relic can be found on the corner of High and Seymons Street.

Blenheim / **Practical Information**

Accommodation

The Blenheim Country Lodge, corner of Alfred and Henry Street, Tel: (3) 578 50 79, rooms for NZ$ 105. *Bings Motel,* centrally located at 29 Maxwell Rd., Tel: (3) 861 99, rooms for NZ$ 66.

Another good motel is *Middle Park Lodge,* 138 Middle Renwick Rd., Tel: (3) 578 33 29, doubles for NZ$ 60, singles for NZ$ 58.

A guest house which can be recommended is the *Koanui Guest House* on Main Street, Tel: (3) 578 74 87. A room with breakfast costs NZ$ 60 for a double and NZ$ 36 for a single.

The selection of campsites for campers and motor homes is good. One can choose between *A1 Motor Camp,* 78 Grove Rd, Tel: (3) 578 36 67, tent site for NZ$ 7 per person, and the *Blenheim Auto Court,* 27 Budge St., Tel: (3) 578 74 19, with prices from NZ$ 6 per night. In addition, there is the *Spring Creek Holiday Park,* located 8 km (5 miles) outside of town toward Picton, Tel: (3) 8 93.

Car Rental: "Avis," 42 Scott Street.

Medical Care: Dr. Deirdre Ahern, 16 Francis Street, Tel: (3) 578 55 99.

Restaurants: Restaurants serving snacks can be found on almost every corner in the centre of town. There are also a number of cafés which serve various lighter meals. Generally speaking, there is no fine dining in Blenheim.

Important Addresses

Information Centre: Corner of Queen and Arthur Street, open weekdays from 9 am to 5 pm.

Police: Police Station, 8 Main Street, Tel: (3) 578 52 79.

Post Office: Located where Main Street meets up with Market and Scott Street.

Camping

The New Zealanders themselves love to travel; therefore, there is an abundance of campsites. Larger cities offer the greatest selection, but even in smaller towns, one will find a suitable spot to pitch a tent. There are also campsites located near the tourist attractions like the national parks. Another widespread option is to rent a cabin, which can accommodate two to eight people. Depending on the size and price category, some are ideal for those who plan to prepare their own meals and backpack travellers, including everything from sleeping bags to kitchen utensils.

There is a sufficient number of sites with the appropriate hook-ups for motor homes as well. One will be quite often be pleasantly surprised by the smaller campsites, which are not only equipped with cozy lobbies and dining rooms with an adjacent kitchen, but with laundry facilities and dryers in addition to the standard sanitary facilities. Even discerning campers will be impressed by the cleanliness of these campsites.

The campsites, located primarily on the outskirts of the city, are also attractive because of their affordable prices: NZ$ 7 per person is the average. However, during peak season from December to February, vacancies can become scarce because the New Zealanders also enjoy travelling and camping during this time of year.

Camping in the wilderness or on a farm does not bother anyone in "Aotearoa," the land of the long white cloud. It is, of course, better to ask the farmer or the owner of the land before pitching a tent. This will almost always lead to a pleasant and interesting conversation allowing insight into the everyday life in New Zealand.

Cape Kidnappers

Located on the eastern coast of the North Island, a few miles south of →*Hastings* is Cape Kidnappers, the name of which is not without justification. In 1769, the Maori attempted to kidnap a Tahitian ship's hand from Captain James Cook's ships. Today, the cape's significance lies elsewhere: it is home to a gannet colony, which is said to be the only colony of this species of migratory bird in the world found on the mainland, located so near to a populated region. The gannet colony is open to the public from November to April, after the offspring have hatched. The colony can be reached on foot. A hike along the steep coastline is definitely worthwhile, but one should check with the Public Relations Office in Napier (Tel: (6) 835 49 49) for information on the tides because this is only possible during low tide. Hiking one way requires covering a distance of 8 kilometres (5 miles). Four-wheel drive jeeps and tractors are another means of reaching the gannet colony.

Cape Reinga →*Ninety Mile Beach*

Car Rental

There are a number of car rental agencies on the North and South Islands. comparing prices will prove beneficial in most cases, especially when renting a motor home. The companies "Maui" in Auckland and Christchurch, "Breakaway" in Auckland, Christchurch, Taupo, Napier and Hastings and "Newman" are especially popular *(→individual entries)*. Other companies like "Rhodes," "Hertz" and "Avis" also offer rental cars at many locations. Although the daily rates for a compact car range from NZ$ 52 to NZ$ 77, a motor home can cost between NZ$ 110 and NZ$ 160. The terms and conditions are similar at all of the agencies: the person renting the vehicle must be 21 or over. Although a national driving licence is sufficient, an international driving licence will expedite the process. As a rule, a deposit of NZ$ 350 to NZ$ 550 is required. This is refundable when the rental vehicle is returned undamaged. The above mentioned prices are daily rates with unlimited mileage. The price for a rental car will often include the services of the →*Automobile Association.* Whether or not a daily insurance fee is charged varies from agency to agency.

Children

New Zealanders are very friendly and hospitable toward children and will be very helpful toward families travelling with children. Unusual illnesses are also not a concern in New Zealand. Many hostels are suited for children. Infants and children under three usually stay in their parents' room free of charge. At campgrounds and in the hotels, children receive a discount of 50%. Children will also receive a discount or free admission to museums, points of interest and other attractions.

Christchurch

Christchurch is one of the loveliest cities in New Zealand and is located in the Otago Region *(→Regions)* on the South Island. Christchurch has the reputation of being one of the most English cities in New Zealand — and the city does live up to its reputation. It is a quiet, picturesque city, located at the base of Port Hill, offering abundant cultural events and an atmosphere quite different from other cities in New Zealand. The city's appearance is orderly and tidy, interrupted by the winding Avon River. A colourful mixture of cultures can be observed here — also a result of the university. The city has a population of about 290,000.

An impressionistic landscape in the light of dusk

Christchurch / **History**

In 1850, the first Europeans arrived here and began building their houses along the banks of the Avon River. These were members of the "Canterbury Society," founded in 1848 in England. The society sent selected members aboard four ships to New Zealand to spread their religious beliefs in Christchurch. However, the members of the "Canterbury Society" had only limited success. The excellent location of Christchurch quickly attracted a large number of shepherds and other immigrants from every country imaginable and secular interests were given priority over the religious.

Christchurch / **Sights**

The best place to begin a tour of the city is at *Cathedral Square*. This is a quaint square in the centre of the city, surrounded by the most impressive buildings and also serving as a meeting place for young and old alike. The *Christchurch Cathedral* is especially beautiful. One can climb the tower and enjoy a panorama of the entire city (open from 9 am to 4 pm). This church was built from 1864 to 1881, and is considered one of the nicest churches in New Zealand. Outstanding elements of the Christchurch Cathedral are: the glass windows, the Selwyn Memorial pulpit and the large wall mosaic.

What will also attract one's attention on Cathedral Square is the beautiful postal building. Those who have more time to spend on the square will most likely make the acquaintance of the *Wizard,* who is just as much a part of Christchurch as the Cathedral itself. Every day, this eccentric looking figure appears in a black robe, often with strange headpieces, with long hair and a beard. He holds speeches directed against just about everything. Although the views he expresses — and quite loudly at that — are questionable at best, abnormal at worst, his "performance" is quite entertaining.

The next point of interest is the *Arts Centre,* located on the corner of Worcester Street and Rollestone Avenue. These former university buildings, built in neo-Gothic architecture relay a pleasant atmosphere with winding passageways, turrets and bay windows opening to the lovely courtyard. Plans to found a university in Christchurch were realised after 25 years in 1873 with the founding of Canterbury College. The number of student increased consistently and the university became too small to accommodate the number of students, making it necessary to spread the students over a number of other campuses. In 1978, the Arts Centre then moved onto the campus, consequently becoming the largest art centre in New Zealand. Here one can visit the numerous studios and observe the artists. It is also possible to buy leather goods, wooden carvings, ceramics and glass, some of which are quite original — others have the character of typical souvenirs. The "Riti Rangi," the Maori carving workshop is also interesting; the artifacts produced here are definitely worth seeing. In addition to the handicrafts store, the Arts Centre also houses four theatres, a gallery, an excellent bookstore, a music store and a dance academy.

Moving out of the bustle of the city, on the opposite side of Rollestone Avenue, is the extensive *Hagley Park* including the *Botanical Gardens*.

It is also quite nice to explore Christchurch by bicycle. The city is laid out in a grid format and has very few hills, making this a good alternative. Another possibility is to rent a boat or canoe and paddle along the Avon River. Another point of interest is the *Orana Park Wildlife Trust,* near the airport on McLeans Island Road. Open daily from 10 am to 5 pm, one can observe the camels, tigers, water buffaloes, zebras and numerous other animals. Admission costs NZ$ 7.

A trip lasting longer, would be an excursion over *Dyers Pass* to →*Banks Peninsula.* Along this route, one will pass *Lyttelton Harbour,* the export harbour of Christchurch. Harbour tours are available.

Christchurch / **Museums and Galleries**

The *Canterbury Museum,* Rollestone Avenue, near the entrance to the botanical garden, features pieces from earlier colonial times. Exhibits includes a reproduction of a Christchurch street during the turn of the century. There are also documents covering the history of the expedition of the Antarctic on display, which is closely linked to Christchurch. The museum is open daily from 10 am to 4:30 pm, admission is free of charge. Directly behind this museum is the *Robert McDougall Art Gallery.* In this gallery, impressive oil paintings by Maori chiefs are on display as well as works by the internationally renowned old masters. There are also newer works by local artists.

Galleries specialising predominantly in New Zealand art include the *CSA Gallery,* 66 Gloucester Street, the *Brooke & Gifford Gallery,* 112 Manchester Street, and the *Ginkgo Gallery* in the Arts Centre.

Christchurch / **Practical Information**

Accommodation

Quality Inn Chateau, Deans Ave., Tel: (3) 48 89 99, singles and doubles NZ$ 175.
Caledonian Hotel, Caledonian Rd., Tel: (3) 66 60 34, singles and doubles NZ$ 72.

Avon Hotel, Oxford Terrace, Tel: (3) 79 11 80, singles NZ$ 88, doubles NZ$ 90. There are a large number of motels in Christchurch. It is best to ask for a current listing at the information centre. Some examples are:

Raceway Motel, 222 Lincoln Rd., Tel: (3) 38 05 11, singles NZ$ 30, doubles NZ$ 44. *Bealey Lodge Guest House,* 69 Bealey Ave., Tel: (3) 66 67 70, singles NZ$ 36, doubles NZ$ 61. Both of these are centrally located. In the stylish, 97 year old *Cockfosters Villa,* Stanmore Rd., Tel: (3) 89 02 06, one will pay NZ$ 30 for a single and NZ$ 55 for a double.

The campsites are all situated outside of the city. Located only 2 miles away is *Addington Showground,* 47 Whiteleigh Rd., Tel: (3) 39 87 70, tent site for NZ$ 5.50. One will pay the same price 6¹/₂ miles away at the campsite *South*

An impressive contrast of old and new — the Bridge of Remembrance in Christchurch

New Brighton Park, Halsey St., Tel: (3) 88 98 44. The *Riccarton Park Motor Camp,* 19 Main South Rd., Tel: (3) 348 56 90, is priced at NZ$ 7.50.

Automobile Association: Office on the corner of Herefort and Madras St.

Beaches: Beautiful beaches can be found about 6¼ miles outside of Christchurch, for example the beaches "South Brighton," "Summer," "North Beach" and "New Brighton."

Car Rental: There are a large number of car rental agencies in Christchurch; the following is only a selection:

"Avis," 94 Gloucester St., "Hertz," 44 Lichfield St. and "Budget Rent-a-Car," on the corner of Oxford Terrace and Lichfield St. "Maui Campavans" is located at 23 Sheffield Crescent; "Newmans," at 530-544 Memorial Ave.; and "Rent-a-Car," at 334 Riccarton Rd.

Entertainment: Whether live music, discotheques, cinemas or theatre — Christchurch has a good selection of free-time activities. Jazz and Rock sessions are performed in *Dux de Lux,* in the Arts Centre or *The Playroom,* corner of Cuff Road and Pages Road. In *Warners,* Cathedral Square, Irish folk

Untamed beauty: the impassible jungles of ferns, palm trees and lush underbrush on the Coromandel Peninsula

music is performed. It is best to obtain information on the current theatre performances at the information centre or in the Arts Centre. Cinemas can be found in the Arts Centre and on Cathedral Square. Churchill offers a number of theatre and ballet performances as well as orchestra concerts.

Medical Care: Christchurch Hospital, Riccarton Ave., Tel: (3) 64 06 40; or City Medical Centre, 784 Colombo St., Tel: (3) 66 61 60.

Restaurants: Christchurch seems to be a paradise for "smorgasbord restaurants." After being seated, one can enjoy the buffet in *Gardens Restaurant,* in the botanical garden or in *The Old Orchard,* 330 Port Hills Road. This is also true for *Town Hall Restaurant,* corner of Kilmore and Colombo Street. A more exclusive restaurant is the *Thomas Edmonds Restaurant,* Cambridge Terrace. New Zealand's first Maori restaurant, the *Te Waka O Maui,* can be found on the corner of Papanui Road and Bealey Avenue. Specialising in fish and seafood is *Fail's Seafood Restaurant,* 82 Cashel Street. Good Italian food can be found at *Tre Gatti's.* 76 Lichfield Street and at *Spagalima's Italian Pizza Restaurant,* 798 Colombo Street. Chinese food is served in *Chung Wah,* 63 Worcester Street. Christchurch also offers a wide selection of vegetarian restaurants. A number of these restaurants enjoy increasing popularity, for example *Dux de Lux* in the Arts Centre or the *Main Street Café,* corner of Colombo Street and Salisbury Road. Numerous cafés and pubs offer snacks in a pleasant atmosphere. Take-away restaurants can also be found everywhere.

Transportation: Airplanes, trains and buses will take visitors from Christchurch to all of the larger and important cities. The connections are very good. Since Christchurch has the second most important airport in New Zealand, international flights also depart from this city.

The public bus system is also well developed; the "Bus Information Office" is located directly on Cathedral Square.

Important Addresses

The *NZTP Office* is situated on Cathedral Square. Here, one can obtain various brochures and other information on the city and its surroundings.

Police: The "District Police Headquarters" is on the corner of Hereford Street and Cambridge Terrace, Tel: (3) 79 39 99.

Post Office: Cathedral Square.

Climate

The seasons in New Zealand are exactly opposite from the seasons on the northern hemisphere. It is dominated by an oceanic climate. On the South

Island, one can encounter cool nights in the summer, dry heat inland, strong winds along the coast and heavy rain showers. The winters are relatively mild, with frost only in the alpine regions. The city of →*Nelson* is known for having the most hours of sunshine during the year. Auckland and the Bay of Islands also have a high proportion of sunny days. Christchurch and the region of Canterbury has the least amount of precipitation on the South Island.

Clothing

Warm articles of clothing and rain gear should be brought along, even when travelling in New Zealand during the summer months. Summer nights — on the South Island especially — can have autumn-like temperatures. Otherwise, shorts, T-shirts, jeans and sport shirts are appropriate attire. The midday heat can get quite intense. Sturdy walking shoes or hiking boots are a must when visiting the national parks in New Zealand. One should limit what is packed to favourite articles of clothing and other necessities because hotels and motels are often equipped with laundry facilities.

Consulates →*Embassies*

Coromandel Peninsula

The beauty of Coromandel Peninsula remains, for the most part, undiscovered by most tourists. It is a rugged section of coast reaching into the Pacific Ocean. Impenetrable jungles of ferns, palms and shrubs paint a fascinating contrast to the ocean and rugged mountains which comprise the Coromandel. This is a paradise for wind surfers and even more so for hikers, who can undertake numerous and interesting expeditions. Whether through the woods or to the gold mines, which make up part of the earlier history of the Coromandel Peninsula, or even through the underbrush, nature presents itself at its best far away from the noise and bustle of civilisation. Secluded beaches and coves offer an inviting setting for swimming and sunbathing. The Coromandel Peninsula can also be explored by car, driving along a rather adventuresome road. The most significant cities and towns on the Coromandel Peninsula are →*Thames, Coromandel* and Waihi.

The city of Coromandel is small and serene. Most of the houses are built in Victorian style. The museum here will also attract the visitors interest, displaying remnants of the gold mining era. It is open daily from 10 am to noon and from

2 to 4 pm. Admission is NZ$ 2. The *Waihi Arts Centre and Museum* in Waihi, a small town built in the style of the wild west, allows insight into the interesting gold rush era. It is open weekdays from 10:30 am to 4 pm, Sundays from 1:30 to 4 pm. Waihi is also renowned as the site of the largest gold vein in New Zealand, which was found in the Martha Mine.

Another highlight of the Coromandel Peninsula is the *Hot Water Beach*. Near the small town of Hahei, one will become acquainted with an interesting phenomenon on this beach along this beautiful coastline. Beneath the sand, hot springs drain into the ocean. In some places, one can dig a hole in the sand and watch it fill up with hot spring water. One should be cautious, however, since the water from these springs is very hot.

Craters of the Moon

The beautiful geothermal area called Craters of the Moon is a fascinating place with hot springs, bubbling mud-pots, the scent of sulphur and ascending trails of steam. This area is open to the public, located 5 km (3 miles) north of →*Taupo.* The better known geothermal park of →*Whakarewarewa,* is in fact larger, but far more crowded as well.

Credit Cards →*Money*

Crime

New Zealand is wonderful for travellers because there is a very low crime rate. It is the exception to the rule that one will fear crime whether travelling by car or backpacking. Of course, when unemployment was on the climb, there were isolated incidents of organised gang violence directed toward tourists. This is no longer the case, but if one should run into trouble then the police should be contacted immediately. Embassies will be of help in cases of lost passports or other emergencies.

Cromwell

Cromwell offers little of interest within a modern-day context. It is located on the main road between →*Queenstown* and →*Wanaka.* However, if one would like to return to the gold rush era, this is just the right place. The confluence of the Chluta and Kawarau Rivers as well as the "Chluta Valley Hydroelectric Power Project" was the site of what was the most important city for the gold trade. Remnants of this era include numerous mining fields, decaying huts and the former water supply system. The *Cromwell Borough Museum* takes visitors back in time to the gold rush era (open daily from 10:30 am to 12:30 pm and from 1:30 to 4:30 pm).

Cromwell / **Practical Information**

Accommodation: *Undersun Park Lodge,* Gair Ave., Tel: (3) 445 03 21, singles NZ$ 38, doubles NZ$45. *Gateway Motel,* Alpha St., Tel: (3) 445 03 85, from NZ$ 28 per person. *Cedar Lodge Motel,* 2 Syndic St., Tel: (3) 445 03 65, singles from NZ$ 25.

One can also camp at the *Sunhaven Motor Camp,* Alpha St., Tel: (3) 445 01 64, NZ$ 6.

Medical Care: Cromwell Hospital, Wanaka Rd., Tel: (03) 4-450-021 or Dr. A. N. Kagan, 33 The Mall, Tel: (3) 445 11 19.

Important Addresses: The *information centre* is located on the street "The Mall," open daily from 9 am to 4 pm.

A paradise for hikers and wind surfers — the rugged coastline of the Coromandel Peninsula

Police: Police Station, Waenga Drive, Tel: (3) 445 19 99.

Cuisine

Those looking for a restaurant with typical New Zealand cuisine will have a very difficult time, although in most pubs, one will find lamb cutlet with potatoes and vegetables on the menu. This is a typical meal in the private households of New Zealand. The various types of fish dishes can be highly recommended, especially at those places located near where the fish are caught. Otherwise, there is a very strong British influence on dining in New Zealand.

International cuisine and fast food can also be found in New Zealand. Chinese food leads in popularity, followed by pizzerias. Indian or Mexican food is also a favourite. For those in a hurry, there are a number of take-aways: small, fast meals which can be eaten on the run. Whether it is fish and chips or a hamburger, New Zealanders have also adapted their eating habits to the quick pace. With some luck, one will find a snack bar or pub along the coast serving fish dishes like the ever-popular crayfish.

Larger cities are a paradise for vegetarians because a number of good restaurants have opened in the past few years.

Wine and beer is not always served in all restaurants. However, many are BYO (bring your own). Licence to serve alcoholic beverages is not granted to many restaurants, but guests can bring their own alcoholic beverages and have it served to them for a small charge.

This is not the case in the numerous pubs where beer flows from the tap in streams. Those who do not like beer, will still find a visit one of these pubs quite interesting. New Zealand wines are also gaining popularity with wine connoisseurs, but good domestic sparkling wines are not easy to find.

Culture

The term "culture" brings the museums and galleries of the larger cities to mind. This is especially true of the famous museums in Auckland and Wellington. In addition to these two museums, others display exhibits pertaining to the colonial times and the Maori culture.

The galleries of New Zealand are also worth visiting, giving not only international artists but local artists, graphic designers and photographers a forum. New Zealand is not renowned for its theatre but it does have a number of ensembles which have attained an international reputation. Most performances take place in larger cities. In addition to the professional theatre ensembles, there are a number of amateur groups.

The New Zealand symphony orchestra and the soprano Kiri Te Kanawa have gained world renown. For jazz fans, the Pacific Eardrum and Colin Hemingson are increasing in popularity. The jazz festival takes place in Tauranga during the Easter season. Many international performances are featured during this festival. Heading the New Zealand pop charts are the groups "Pink Flamingos, "Split Enz" and "Dance Exponents."

The cultural scene is also characterised by diverse handicrafts from pottery to wood carvings and even jade jewellry.

Currency →*Money*

Customs Regulations

Articles for personal use may be brought into the country including: photographic equipment and ten rolls of film. In addition, 200 cigarettes or 250 grams of tobacco or 50 cigars, 4.5 litres of wine or beer and 1.1 litre of liquor. Importing plants, seeds, meat, fish, fruit, soil and sand are strictly prohibited and this is also checked carefully. It is also possible that camping and hiking equipment must be thoroughly disinfected upon arrival.

Dargaville

The otherwise colourless city of Dargaville does make a good point of depar-ture for a tour through the →*Waipoua Kauri Forest*. The *Northern Wairoa Museum* serves as a reminder of the prosperous times in Dargaville, when it was an important commercial centre for the wood industry as well as being a busy harbour town. The museum displays interesting exhibits pertaining to the Maori culture including a canoe used in battle from the era before Euro-pean settlement. Also in the museum are displays of Kauri workmanship as well as everything else having to do with navigation. The museum is located in Harding Park on a small knoll, 3 km (2 miles) outside the city. In front of the museum is the mast of the most famous Greenpeace ship, the "Rainbow Warrior," which serves as a reminder of the terrorist bomb attack in 1985, when the ship was anchored in the harbour of Auckland.

A visit to Dargaville is worthwhile mainly because of the beautiful beaches, which can, by all means, compete with the →*Ninety Mile Beach* in appearance

Dargaville / **Practical Information**

Accommodation: *Northern Wairoa Hotel,* Hokianga Rd., Tel: 89 23, from NZ$ 30 per person.

Commercial Hotel, River Rd., Tel: 80 18, is available at the same price.

Awakino Point Lodge Motel, SH 14, Tel: 78 70, singles NZ$ 55, doubles NZ$ 68. The *Dargaville Youth Hostel,* Tel: 6-342, corner of Portland and Gordon Street costs NZ$ 11 per night. One can also camp at the *Selwyn Park,* Tel: 82 86, for NZ$ 6; small cottages are also available as are sites for motor homes.

Restaurants: One restaurant worth visiting is in the *Northern Wairoa Hotel,* offering excellent cuisine.

Important Addresses: Information is available at a small newsstand on Normanby Street.

Discounts

An international student identity card is accepted in almost all of the museums, entitling the holder to discounts of up to 50%. There will almost always be a children's discount, and for things like visits to the museum, admission for children will usually be free.

Doubtful Sound →*National Parks: Fjordland National Park*
Driving Licence →*Travel Documents*

Dunedin

The harbour city of Dunedin is commonly referred to as "the Edinburgh of the south." During the gold rush era, this city was an important centre for transport; today, the city sooner leaves a tranquil impression. However, the weather here is often cool and variable. Despite this, a visit to this, the second largest city on the South Island, is definitely worthwhile. The first university in New Zealand, Otago University, was founded in Dunedin in 1869.

Dunedin / **History**

Members of the Free Scottish Church founded Dunedin in 1848. They built the city in their typical style, the buildings having numerous gables, bay windows and turrets. Of course, this idyllic Protestant setting was to end with the

---

The painstaking carvings on this storage hut are typical of every Maori village ▶

first discovery of gold in Otago. During the gold rush, Dunedin became the wealthiest city in the most affluent province of New Zealand. During the height of the gold rush in 1863, Dunedin became the economic capital of the country. Numerous prospectors settled here changing the profile of this city tremendously. In addition to the magnificent trade centres and banks, casinos, brothels and bars also sprang up all over the city. Today, there is not much left of this more or less "wild" chapter in Dunedin's history. The university attracts more than 6,000 students to Dunedin, making up a part of this city's cultural flair. The local residents live mainly from agriculture.

Dunedin / **Sights**

The centre of Dunedin is laid out in the form of an octagon, making all of the sights worth visiting quite easy to find. Many of the buildings are built in Victorian style, characteristic of the Dunedin's "golden age." Examples of this are *Saint Paul's Anglican Cathedral* and the police station. The abundance of parks give Dunedin its special appeal; most highly recommended are the *Botanical Gardens* on Great Kings Street. A visit to the "Cadbury Chocolate Factory" offers a welcome change to the usual sightseeing tours. This can booked through the visitors centre.

Dunedin / **Museums and Galleries**

Early Settlers Museum, at 220 Cumberland Street, brings the visitor closer to that period in time when this region was first settled. There are, however, other exhibits in this museum pertaining to other interesting historical periods, for example, an exhibit on the history and techniques of whaling. The museum is open weekdays from 9 am to 4:30 pm, Saturdays from 10:30 am to 4:30 pm and Sundays from 1:30 to 4:30 pm; admission NZ$ 3.50.

The *Otago Museum,* on the corner of Great King and Union Street, provides insight into specific aspects into the Maori culture as well as Pacific cultures in general. It is open weekdays from 9 am to 4:30 pm, Saturdays from 10:30 am to 4:30 pm and Sundays from 1:30 to 4:30 pm. Admission is free of charge. The *Art Gallery* is the oldest gallery in New Zealand, located in Logan Park on Anzac Avenue on the outskirts of the city. Works by international and local artists can be viewed here daily from 10 am to 4:30 pm and during weekends from 2 to 5 pm.

Dunedin / **Practical Information**

Accommodation

Dunedin's hotels in the luxury category include the *Southern Cross,* 118 High St., Tel: (3) 477 07 52, singles and doubles NZ$ 123, and the *Quality Inn,* Upper Moray Place, Tel: (3) 477 67 84, with singles and doubles priced from NZ$ 130. Both hotels are centrally located. Another nice hotel can be found on the corner of Cumberland and High St., the *Leviathan Hotel,* Tel: (3) 477 31 60, with singles for NZ$ 63 and doubles for NZ$ 68. Additional addresses: *Wharf Hotel,* 25 Fryatt St., Tel: (3) 477 12 33, singles from NZ$ 30; *Wains Hotel,* Princes St., Tel: (3) 477 92 83, singles NZ$ 67, doubles NZ$ 85; *Beach Motel,* corner of Prince Albert and Victoria Rd., Tel: (3) 455 50 43, singles NZ$ 73, doubles NZ$ 79.

Guest Houses: *Magnolia House,* Grindon St., Tel: (3) 477 19 99, singles NZ$ 30, doubles NZ$ 60 including breakfast and *Sahara Guest House,* near the university, 619 George St., Tel: (3) 477 66 62, singles NZ$ 40, doubles NZ$ 60 including breakfast. The *Kinnaird House,* 97 Moray Place, Tel: (3) 477 67 81, offers more modest accommodation with singles priced at NZ$ 30, doubles at NZ$ 40 including breakfast.

The *Stafford Gables Youth Hostel,* 71 Stafford St., Tel: 741-919 costs NZ$ 13 per person per night. The *YMCA* is located at 54 Moray Place, Tel: (3) 477 95 55, costing NZ$ 15 per night. The same price is charged by the guest house *Elm Lodge,* 74 Elm Rd., Tel: (3) 474 18 72.

The three camping sites all have sites for motor homes as well as offering rental cottages: *Aaron Lodge Motor Camp,* 162 Kaikorai Rd., Tel: (3) 647 25, tent sites from NZ$ 6 per person. *Leith Valley Touring Park,* 103 Malvern St., Woodhaugh, Tel: (3) 741 936, from NZ$ 7. *Tahuna Park Seaside Camp,* near the beach at Saint Kilda, Tel: (3) 546 90, from NZ$ 6.

Automobile Association: 450 Moray Place, open Monday to Friday from 8:30 am to 5 pm.

Car Rental: "Rent-a-Car," 124 St. Andrew Street; "Avis," 25 Stafford Street.

Entertainment: The number of pubs in Dunedin will ensure that the evenings never become boring. Most of the well-frequented are the bars in the various hotels like *Prince of Wales,* 474 Princes Street, the *Provincial,* 6 Stafford Street or *Law Courts Establishment,* corner of Stuart and Cumberland Street. One will, of course, discover a lot more cozy alternatives during a stroll through the streets of Dunedin. Some of the bars offer live entertainment like in *Beach Hotel* on Kilda Street and in *Hotel Branson,* 91 Saint Andrew's Street. In addition, Dunedin has three cinemas.

Medical Care: Dunedin Hospital, 201 Great Kind St., Tel: (3) 474 09 99 or Dr. James Hanon, Hansborough House, 112 Moray Place, Tel: (3) 477 09 61.

Restaurants: An excellent Mexican restaurant, *Los Gatos,* is located at 199 Stuart Street. One must, however, bring along a good portion of patience since it can take up to a half an hour to be seated. Those who view this positively will consider it a good sign for the quality of the food. A restaurant in which one will be seated much more quickly, but which is also much more expensive is *Blades,* 450 George Street. A selection of vegetarian dishes is available in *Terrace Café,* 118 Moray Place. *Palms Café,* located on the corner of High and Dowling Street, offers everything from delicious salads to snacks to complete meals at reasonable prices.

A number of good snack bars can be found on Moray Place as well as on George Street. Vegetarian dishes are also available in *Ma Cuisine,* 45 Moray Place as well as at the *Sidewalk Café,* 480 Moray Place.

Those interested in a quick, tasty meal can find what they're looking for at *The Upper Crust,* 263 George Street and *Partners,* 351 George Street.

Those preferring a colourful atmosphere will enjoy the student café *Captain Cook,* on the corner of Albany and Great King Street.

Dunedin has a much wider selection of cafés and restaurants than can be listed here. Therefore, it is worthwhile to get the brochure "Eating Out in Dunedin" from the visitors centre.

Transportation

Bus

"Newman's Coach Services" as well as the public NZRRS routes offer cross-country connections. The Newman office is located at 205 Andrew Street; the NZRRS bus terminal is on Cumberland Street.

Train

Dunedin has good rail connections to all of the significant destinations. The train station is on Anzac Avenue.

Air Travel

A large number of domestic flights to both larger and smaller cities depart from Dunedin (→*Travel in New Zealand).* The bus to the airport departs from the visitors centre on the Octagon.

Important Addresses

NZTP Information Centre: 123 Prince St., open from 8:30 am to 5 pm.

Dunedin Visitor's Centre: 48 The Octagon, Monday to Friday from 8:30 am to 5 pm, Saturdays and Sundays from 9 am to 5 pm.
Police: Dunedin Central Police Station, Lower High St., Tel: (3) 477 60 11.
Post Office: Corner of Princes and Water Street.

Economy

The main branch of the economy is agriculture, primarily the breeding of sheep and cattle. The main crops raised in New Zealand are feed plants, potatoes, vegetables, fruit, corn and grains. The fishing industry also plays a significant role in New Zealand. Export goods are predominantly meat, dairy products and wool (New Zealand is a leader in the export of wool on the world market). Until the last decade when large scale industrialisation took place, New Zealand had always been an agriculturally based economy. The food industry is the leading industry in New Zealand followed by the wood and the automobile industries.

Electricity

New Zealand has alternating current, 230/240 volts, 50 hertz. Campsites, hotels and motels also are equipped with tripolar sockets and 110 volts.

Embassies

The United States Embassy
29 Fitzherbert Terrace
P.O. Box 1190
Thorndon, Wellington
New Zealand
Tel: (0644) 472-2068

British High Commission
44 Hill Street
Wellington 1
New Zealand
Tel: (0644) 472-6049

Emergency

The emergency number for the police, fire department or ambulance is 111. Fast assistance can be expected in all emergencies. Specific numbers for local emergency services can be found on the first page of the local telephone books.

Entertainment

Many find the New Zealand night life to be a bit short. The pubs close at 10 pm. Discotheques and international bars can mainly be found in the tourist centres like →*Queenstown.* Here, one can enjoy the night life well into the wee hours of the morning. Otherwise, the cinema and theatre are also options in a large number of cities.

Equipment

Even during the New Zealand summertime, a warm sweater will be an essential travel companion. Rain gear is equally appropriate. Those who want to enjoy the beauty of the individual national parks will need sturdy shoes (hiking boots are recommended). One should also bring along a small backpack to stow the necessary equipment for outings.

Ferries →*Travel in New Zealand*

Folklore

Those interested in the original folklore of New Zealand should best seek contact to the Maori. The Maori are the original inhabitants of New Zealand, from Polynesian origin. To gain the most insight into the Maori culture, one should visit the museum village of →*Whakarewarewa* near → *Rotorua.* Here, one can experience the culture of the South Pacific, including war and rain dances, the harmonic and aggressive rhythms and the traditional costumes. Visitors will gain valuable information on the sagas and legends, which the Maori have handed down over the centuries. One opportunity to experience the original folklore of the country is to visit one of the "Maori evenings" in one of the hotels. This will more than likely be the first time that visitors experience the well known nose rubbing, the hangi, the customary Maori greeting. In addition to the hotels, now and then, there are concerts held in some of the museums, for example in Auckland and Wellington.

Fox Glacier

The longer and more famous of the two glaciers in New Zealand is Fox Glacier stretching from the heights of Mount Cook to the coastal regions. It is located on the western side of the South Island. Short and easy hikes to the mass of ice are popular as are helicopter tours. Organised expeditions to the glacier are also offered which are combined with a trip by light aircraft making it possible to get extremely close to the glacier.

Fox Glacier / **Practical Information**
Accommodation
The *Fox Glacier Hotel* offers accommodation for NZ$ 62 for a single room and NZ$ 80 for a double room, Tel: 308 39. Charging NZ$ 59 per person is the *Golden Glacier Motor Inn,* 6 State Highway, Tel: 308 47. Located somewhat outside the village heading toward Lake Matheson is the *Fox Glacier Motor Park,* Tel: 308 21. This is a very well equipped campsite. A tent site costs NZ$ 6, cabins start at NZ$ 12.

Restaurants: The selection of restaurants is not immense in this small village, but visitors will not go hungry. The *Fox Glacier Hotel,* offers breakfast and hot meals, but it is rather expensive. Another possibility is the *Fox Glacier Restaurant and Tearoom.*

Important Addresses
The *Information Centre* is located in the centre of the village and is open from 8 am to 5 pm daily. In addition to detailed information about Fox Glacier, tours offered (both long and short) or direct booking of glacier flights, a slide show on the glacier is also presented.

Franz Josef Glacier
Located 25 kilometres (16 miles) north of →*Fox Glacier,* its "little brother" Franz Josef Glacier stretches through the mountains into the flatlands. This site is just as impressive as Fox Glacier.

Franz Josef Glacier / **Practical Information**
Accommodation
Just outside of the centre of town in the *THC Franz Josef,* Tel: 719, one will pay NZ$ 73 per person per night. The guest house *Callery Lodge,* Cron Street, Tel: 738, charges NZ$ 26 for a single room and NZ$ 40 for a double room. In the same area is the *Franz Josef Youth Hostel* at 2 Cron Street, Tel: 754. The hostile is comfortable and clean costing only NZ$ 12 per person.

In addition, there is a campsite in this area: *Franz Josef Motor Camp.* It is located somewhat outside of town, Tel: 742. Tent sites cost NZ$ 5.50, cottages NZ$ 10 per person, accommodation in the adjacent motel cost NZ$ 68 for singles and doubles.

Medical Care: Franz Josef Surgery, Tel: (028-831) 700.

Restaurants: The *THC Franz Josef,* in the *HA Restaurant and Tearoom* and *Glacier Store and Tearoom* offer warm meals. These meals are, however, quite expensive due to the number of tourists who visit Franz Josef Glacier.

Important Addresses: Directly in town is the *Westland National Park Information Centre,* open daily from 8 am to 5 pm.

Fuel

Diesel and lead-free fuel are available everywhere in New Zealand. Higher octanes are also readily available, even in the rural regions. Diesel costs around 74 cents; normal fuel, around 88 cents; and super, around 90 cents per litre.

Geography

New Zealand lies between the 34th and 47th degree of latitude and the 166th and 179th degree of longitude in the southern hemisphere. The North, South and Stuart Islands are a total of 1600 kilometres (1,000 miles) in length. Numerous, mostly uninhabited islands surround the main islands and also belong to the territory of New Zealand. The country is roughly 269,070 square kilometres (103,887 square miles) in area. The main islands are separated by the Cook Strait and are bordered on the west coast by the Tasman Sea, and on the east coast by the Pacific Ocean.

The South Island is about 151,000 square kilometres (58,301 square miles) and is topographically similar to the southern Alps. The island is in part covered by glaciers and the highest peak is Mount Cook, reaching an altitude of 3,764 metres (12,308 feet). The southern portion of the island is comprised of the Fjordlands and in the east are the Canterbury Plains.

The North Island covers an approximate area of 115,000 square kilometres (44,402 square miles). It is less mountainous than the South Island, comprised of rolling hills. The landscape is volcanic with hot springs, geysers and mud pots. Several of the volcanoes are still active.

Gisborne

One will find a sunny climate and beautiful beaches on the east coast of the North Island around Gisborne. Gisborne is not a culturally spectacular city,

The shimmering grey and white of Fox Glacier ▶

but it makes a good place to unwind and enjoy excursions to the nearby hot springs and waterfalls.

Gisborne / **History**

The European settlers gave Gisborne a wide berth for quite a while. This region was first settled at the end of the 19th century. Today, Gisborne is a residential and trade centre. Captain James Cook did, however, land here when he first arrived in New Zealand on October 9, 1769. Despite the widespread unrest among the various Maori tribes in 1860, the proportion of Maori in the population of Gisborne remains considerably high.

Gisborne / **Sights**

This city is distinguished by the many beautiful parks and gardens as well as the idyllic promenades. Other than this, this easternmost city in New Zealand is known for the cultivation of fruit and vegetables as well as the outstanding wines. Worth seeing is the bronze statue of James Cook at the base of Kaiti Hill and the monument to "Little Nick" in the Churchill Park. Little Nick was the ship hand who was the first of the crew to spot New Zealand.

Gisborne / **Museums and Galleries**

Although there are a numbers of museums of navigation in New Zealand, the *Maritime Museum* on Stout Street is definitely worth seeing. The museum is actually a 12,000 ton ship which ran aground here in 1912. It was so heavily damaged, that it would never sail again, laying in a dilapidated condition for several years until the daughter of the second owner restored it for the simple reason that housing was scarce. Upon her death, she left her now famous home to the city of Gisborne, which made it into a museum. The museum contains primarily objects from stranded ships, exhibitions pertaining to whale hunts and Maori art and canoes. The Maritime Museum is open weekdays from 10 am to 4 pm and weekends from 2 pm to 4:30 pm. Admission is NZ\$ 3. The *Gisborne Museum & Art Gallery* is also worth a visit. The history of the Maori, the era of colonisation and the development of the country is presented here. Along with a considerable collection of Maori art, national and international artists are also represented here. The gallery is open Tuesday to Thursday from 10 am to 4 pm and Saturday and Sunday from 12:30 to 4:30 pm. Admission is NZ\$ 2.

Gisborne / **Practical Information**

Accommodation

The selection of accommodation in Gisborne is quite large, even in the centre of town. *Orange Grove Hotel,* 549 Childers Rd., Tel: (6) 876 99 78, open all year, singles and doubles NZ$ 69. *Wainui Motel,* 34 Wairere Rd., Tel: (6) 868 58 82, singles NZ$ 56, doubles NZ$ 65. *Colonial Motor Lodge,* 715 Gladstone Rd., Tel: (6) 867 91 65, singles and doubles NZ$ 88. *Green Gables Guest House,* 31 Rawiri St., Tel: (6) 867 98 72 offers a nice atmosphere including breakfast at NZ$ 35 for single rooms and NZ$ 59 for double rooms. Located centrally is the *Channels Private Hostel,* corner of Gladstone Road and Peel Street, Tel: (6) 867 50 37, singles NZ$ 20, doubles NZ$ 40.

About two kilometres (1¼ miles) outside of town across the river is the *Gisborne Youth Hostel,* 32 Harris St., Tel: (6) 632 69, charging NZ$ 11.

As an exception to the rule, in Gisborne the camping sites are located relatively centrally. *Waikanae Beach Municipal Camp,* Grey St., Tel: (6) 867 56 34, priced at NZ$ 9 per person and NZ$ 16 for cottages. Also near the city and beach is the *Churchill Park Municipal Camp,* Salisbury Rd., Tel: (6) 867 45 55, offering only tent sites for NZ$ 9.

Automobile Association: The office is located on the corner of Disraeli Street and Palmerston Road.

Car Rental: "Avis," 247 Palmerston Road.

Entertainment: Disco and live music can be found in the night club "Silver Lair." Also, come of the hotels offer live music during weekends.

Medical Care: Gisborne Hospital, Ormond Rd., Tel: (6) 867 90 99 or Desmond Road Medical Centre, Desmond Rd., Tel: (6) 867 90 27.

Restaurants: The restaurant *Arnhem* is located directly on the banks of the river, offering very good, although expensive cuisine. Also serving excellent food is the *Bread and Roses* on the corner of Lowe and Reads Quay. Those who prefer fish should try the *Lyric Café,* 124 Gladstone Road.

Shopping: The *Maori Arts & Crafts Centre* is located at 31 Gladstone Street, offering far more than beautiful wood carvings

Transportation: There are good air, rail and bus connections in Gisborne. The bus terminal is on the corner of Bright Street and Childers Road.

Important Addresses

Information is available at the Public Relations Office, 209 Grey Street, open Monday to Friday from 9 am to 5 pm and Saturdays from 10 am to 1 pm.

Police: Gisborne Police Station, Peel St., Tel: (6) 867 90 59.
Post Office: corner of Grey Street and Palmerston Road.

Greymouth

The city of Greymouth lies on the South Island and makes up the economic centre of the western coast. The wood trade flourishes here. The charm of this sleepy little city with about 12,000 residents is the interesting coastline. Here, one will discover rugged and secluded sections. Especially beautiful is the 40 kilometre (25 mile) trip to the →*Pancake Rocks* in Punakaiki.

Greymouth / **History**

For a long time, only Maori lived in this jade-rich region. In 1860, during the gold rush, Greymouth was founded as a prospectors' settlement. → *Shantytown,* a restored gold mining town, is a relic from this era. Shantytown can be toured.

Greymouth / **Sights**

The city itself has little to offer, but dies make a good point of departure for excursions like a drive to Pancake Rocks or Shantytown, a boat trip on the Grey River or a tour around the city on horseback. Information on these activities is available at the Information Office.

Greymouth / **Practical Information**

Accommodation

The *Duke of Edinburgh Hotel,* Guiness St., Tel: (3) 768 40 20, singles and doubles NZ$ 59. *Ashley Hotel,* Tasman St., Tel: (3) 768 51 35, singles NZ$ 90, doubles NZ$ 99.

A centrally located guest house is the *Golden Coast Guest House,* 10 Smith St., Tel: (3) 768 78 39, singles NZ$ 48, doubles NZ$ 68.

The *Greymouth Youth Hostel,* Cowper St., Tel: (3) 768 49 51, charges NZ$ 11 per night.

Located somewhat outside of Greymouth are the two camping sites, both south of town. About three kilometres (2 miles) away on Chesterfield St., is the *Greymouth Seaside Motor Camp,* Tel: (3) 768 66 18. Tent sites start at NZ$ 6; cottages, NZ$ 20. Five kilometres (3 miles) away is the *South Beach Motel,* Main South Rd., Tel: (3) 277 68, singles NZ$ 51, doubles NZ$ 62.

Car Rental: "Avis," 17 Tarapui Street.

Medical Care: Greymouth Hospital, Water Walk, Tel: (3) 768 04 99 or Dr. J. Eakin, 179 Tainui St., Tel: (3) 768 59 02.

Restaurants: The selection in Greymouth is not exactly overwhelming. Snacks and light meals can be found in most pubs and cafés. The *West Inn* on Main South Road is recommended for those who enjoy fish.

Transportation: There are buses and trains connecting Greymouth with other cities and points of interest like the glaciers. The buses to Christchurch are especially good.

Important Addresses

Greymouth Information Office in Regent Theatre, corner of Mackay and Herbert Street, open weekdays from 9 am to 5 pm.

Police: Police Station, Tarapuki Street, Tel: (3) 768 03 36.

Post Office: Corner of Guiness and Albert Street.

One of the typical New Zealand houses along the promenade in Gisborne

Hamilton

The largest city within the interior of the North Island, about 100 km (63 miles) south of Auckland, is Hamilton with its population of 98,000. Hamilton is situated on the longest river in the country, the Waikato River. Over the years, it has become one of the richest agricultural areas. As a university city, it is also famous for its agricultural research centres.

Hamilton / **Sights**

Hamilton is a city which is first and foremost suited as a point of departure for trips into the surrounding regions due to its location. Unfortunately, the city itself offers little for tourists. What can be recommended is a long boat trip along the Waikato River, a visit to "Farmhouse," where one can observe the shearing of sheep (demonstrated daily) with an abundance of information on raising sheep also available. One can also visit the Hilldale Zoo Park, about 8 km (5 miles) outside the city.

Hamilton / **Practical Information**

Accommodation

The *Commercial Establishment,* Victoria St., Tel: (7) 839 12 26, offers accommodation in double and single rooms priced from NZ$ 40. However, since Hamilton has the largest concentration of motels in New Zealand, selecting one becomes difficult. There are also numerous guest houses, for instance *Parklands Travel Hotel,* 24 Bridge St., Tel: (7) 836 24 61, singles NZ$ 35, doubles NZ$ 71 and the *Eastwood Manor,* 209 Grey St., Tel: (7) 856 90 29, singles and doubles NZ$ 84.

The *Hamilton Youth Hostel* is located at 1190 Victoria St., Tel: (7) 836 00 09, NZ$ 11 per night. The *YMCA,* corner of Pembroke and Clarence Street, Tel: (7) 836 22 18 is somewhat more expensive, priced at NZ$ 14.

The camping site *Municipal Camp,* Ruakura Rd., Tel: (7) 582 55, charges NZ$ 8 per night. The *Hamilton East Tourist Court,* Tel: (7) 856 62 20 can be found on Cameron Road in the eastern portion of Hamilton, with tent sites priced at NZ$ 6.50 and cottages from NZ$ 13 per person.

Automobile Association: Anglesea Street.

Car Rental: "Avis" at 342 Barton Street.

Entertainment: Hamilton's night life is somewhat more pronounced than is otherwise the case in New Zealand thanks to the numerous students. Various taverns like *Tavern Hillcrest,* corner of York and Clyde Street, *Chartwell Tavern* and *Eastside Tavern* offer live music almost every evening. Disco music can be heard in *Uncle Sam's,* Ward Street, and *Shakes,* 30 Alexandra Street, offers a broad spectrum of entertainment.

Medical Care: Waikato Hospital, Pembroke St., Tel: (7) 839 88 99 or Hamilton Medical & Injury Centre, 130 Rostrevar St., Tel: (7) 838 03 00.

Restaurants: In Hamilton there is a large selection of restaurants. For example, in *No. 8,* at 8 Alma Street, one can enjoy excellent Italian food, while the *Singapore Restaurant* on Garden Place is one of the numerous restaurants serving excellent Chinese food. Mexican food is available at *Eldorado,* 10 Alma Street, and exquisite cuisine is served in *Anderson's,* 104 London Street. There are pubs and take-aways on almost every corner of Hamilton, offering good and inexpensive food.

Important Addresses

Information is available at the *Waikato Visitor Information Centre,* 865 Victoria St., open weekdays from 9 am to 4:30 pm, Saturdays from 9 am to noon.

Police: Central Police Station, Bridge Street, Tel: (7) 838-09 89.

Post Office: Victoria Street, facing the river.

Hanmer Springs

In the northern part of the South Island, halfway between Greymouth and Christchurch, one will discover the small health resort of Hanmer Springs. Hanmer Springs is surrounded by lofty, wooded peaks. Its 900 residents enjoy a laid-back atmosphere. One can hike through the surrounding areas or simply unwind. The hot spring have a therapeutic effect. The reputation of this town began to develop in 1859, and by 1883, the area was primarily a health resort. Hanmer Springs is the largest thermal spa on the South Island, providing ample opportunity to hike, swim, fish and to ski during the winter.

Hanmer Springs / **Practical Information**

Accommodation: Motels and guest houses are available in Hanmer Springs, for example the *Shining Cuckoo,* Cheltenham St., Tel: (3) 315 70 95, singles NZ$ 37, doubles NZ$ 62 or the *Green Acres Motel,* Conical Hill Rd., Tel: (3) 315 71 25, singles and doubles NZ$ 68.

Restaurants: Since this area is not heavily frequented by tourists, there is only one restaurant in Hanmer Springs near the small post office: the *Alpine Restaurant.*

Hastings

The small, quiet city of Hastings is overshadowed by its "sister city" Napier, located 21 km (13 miles) away. Beautifully situated on Hawkes' Bay, the inner city of Hastings is characterised by Art Deco architecture. This was the result of a dramatic event of nature: in 1931, a massive earthquake almost completely destroyed Hastings. At the time of reconstruction, the Art Deco style was in fashion.

Hastings / **Sights**

Most worthwhile is a leisurely stroll through the inner city of Hastings, so that one can become familiar with this highly individual architectural style. A nice alternative to the normal sightseeing tours in other cities is a visit to the wine cellars of Hastings, renowned for the best wines in New Zealand. A visit to *Fantasyland* in Windsor Park is also quiet fun. What is especially impressive here are the replicas of old English towns which served as settings for many fairy tales. An excursion to →*Cape Kidnappers* is also worthwhile.

Hastings / **Practical Information**
Accommodation

Accommodation can be found at *Fantasyland Motel,* corner of Sylvan Road and Jervois Street, Tel: (6) 876 81 59, singles NZ$ 63, doubles NZ$ 71 or at *Aladdin Lodge,* 120 Maddison St., Tel: (6) 876 67 36, singles NZ$ 52, doubles NZ$ 65.

Car Rental: "Breakaway Motorhomes" on Road 11.

Medical Care: Memorial Hospital, Omahu Rd., Tel: (6) 878 81 09 or Hawkes' Bay Health Service, 110 Russell St., Tel: (6) 876 84 45.

Transportation: Airplanes, trains and busses connect Hastings with all of the important cities.

Important Addresses

Police: Hastings Police Station, Railway Road, Tel: (6) 878 30 07.

History

The early history of the →*Aotearoa* islands go back to approximately 750 A.D., when the Moriori, not to be confused with the existing Maori, came to the islands. Even today the Moriori are known as the Moa hunters. These people lived predominantly on the South Island but also along the western coast of the North Island. They lived from hunting the flightless Moa birds. These were similar to the ostrich; unfortunately, they have long since become extinct. However, the history of these early inhabitants has only recently been verified through archaeological excavations.

More in-depth is the research concerning the Maori, who, even today, are considered the original inhabitants of New Zealand. According to legends, the Polynesian navigator Kupe discovered New Zealand around 950 A.D. Kupe did not first see the islands, but a large white cloud over them. Kupe was so inspired by this, that he named it →*Aotearoa* and then travelled back to Hawaiki. Hawaiki is the legendary homeland of the Maori. However, its exact location remains a mystery.

Four centuries after this discovery, the Maori took possession of this land. Over-population and the consequent food shortages forced the Maori to leave Hawaiki.

The Maori left their homeland in ten large canoes to arrive in New Zealand. To this day, the names of the ten canoes are used as the tribal names of the Maori. The history and legends of this great journey to New Zealand is kept alive through Maori songs and dances.

The Maori were not only hunters and fishers but also cultivated the fertile land. The imported several species of plants as well, including the Kumara (sweet potato). In New Zealand, the Maori quickly developed their own culture, greatly influenced by their Polynesian origins. For this reason, forms of cannibalism were common, for both nutritional and ritualistic reasons. Since the Maori never developed a written language, they used wood carvings as a medium of communication. These carvings were the origins of the elaborate carvings on the war canoes and assembly halls. Even the different types of tattoos worn by men and women date back to these times (→*Whakarewarewa*).

It is written that New Zealand was discovered in 1642 by the Dutch navigator Abel Tasman. According to recorded history, he landed on the island, only to leave quickly after several of his crew fell victim to cannibalism. From this point, the existence of New Zealand was known but it would take more than a century before the British would occupy the islands.

Captain James Cook had more luck with the inhabitants of →*Aotearoa* when he landed in 1769. At first, Cook met a hostile reception from the Maori but thanks to a Tahitian crew member, he was able to make friendly contact and go ashore on his second attempt. Cook wasted no time in claiming the entire country for the British crown. After Cook made this claim public, interest spread rapidly in America and Europe. The first to begin the economic exploitation of New Zealand were the seal hunters. The whaling also grew rapidly in importance. However, for those who preferred dry land under their feet soon learned the profitability of exporting Kauri wood (→*Waipoua Kauri Forest*). Even though the land was systematically exploited, the pakehas (European settlers) could maintain good relations with Maori. Barter began and the Maori learned a great deal of agricultural techniques. Guns and alcohol were no longer foreign to the Maori. This coexistence escalated at the beginning of the 19th century. The European settlers, still a minority at the time, brought along unknown diseases and plagues. However, the Maori population was not only reduced by these diseases but also by tribal feuds. The effect of these feuds was furthered by the firearms, which most of them possessed by this time. The first missionaries to land at the Bay of Islands in 1814, under the leadership of Samuel Marsden (the founder of the first mission in New Zealand), were not confronted with an easy task. However, as the Maori realised the advantages offered by the missionaries — not in changing their beliefs, but through the knowledge of science and crafts — their relationship grew friendlier.

In 1832, New Zealand was officially declared a British colony. This was done in order to protect the Maori people and culture, but the primary concern of the British crown was to establish trading rights. In 1840, Captain William Hobson was sent to New Zealand as the first governor to negotiate the agreements with the Maori leaders. With the help of James Busby, responsible for justice and order during the colonisation, negotiations took place in Waitangi on the Bay of Islands. The treaty was agreed upon and translated into the Maori language. It continued the right of the Maori to retain their land but also gave the British preemptive rights to these regions. The Maori recognised the British as the head of state with the signing of this treaty. In exchange, the Maori were promised the privilege of British citizenship. The treaty was signed by 46 Maori chiefs and the representative of the British crown on February 6, 1840. Since this time, February 6 is celebrated as "Treaty of Waitangi" — a national holiday.

This is when the actual exploitation of the Maori culture began. Their land, which they had sold for little money, was then sold to new settlers for much higher sums. The "New Zealand Company" began a systematically planned colonisation of the regions according to the blueprints of its founder Edward Gibbon Wakefields. Countless settlers found a new home in New Zealand. The settlers worked the land, but also fell into conflict with the Maori, who felt betrayed by these new developments.

After the first seals and whales were hunted, and after the Kauri trees had been cleared, there was little left that ensured the profitability of New Zealand. The country was then flooded with Australian sheep. Powerful land owners settled mainly on the South Island.

Hokitika

The city of Hokitika, 40 kilometres (25 miles) south of →*Greymouth,* was once a centre for prospecting. Today, in contrast, precious stones are processed here. This type of craftsmanship can be observed in some of the shops. Likewise, glass blowers have also settled into Hokitika. With the exception of these groups, this small town lives from the lumber industry. One can learn quite a lot about the gold era in the *West Coast Historical Museum,* Tancred Street. The museum is open Monday to Friday from 9:30 am to 4:30 pm, weekends from 2 to 4:30 pm; admission NZ$ 2.50.

Hokitika / **Practical Information**

Accommodation: *Tudor Motel,* Tudor St., Tel: 581 93, singles and doubles NZ$ 59 or *Southland Hotel,* Revell St., Tel: 583 44, singles NZ$ 72, doubles NZ$ 82. The quaint *Central Guest House,* 20 Hamilton St., Tel: 582 32 offers single rooms for NZ$ 29 and double rooms for NZ$ 44.

Car Rental: "Avis" on Stefford Street.

Medical Care: Westland Hospital, Fitzherbert St., Tel: 587 40 or Dr. L.R. Kitson, 54 Sewell St., Tel: 581 80.

Restaurants: *Chez Pierre* in the Railway Hotel on Sewell Street has a large selection of good and reasonably priced meals. The *Westland Hotel* also serves good food. Other than this, various snacks can be found in a number of shops and tearooms.

Shopping: Those who like jade jewellry will find a wide selection in Hokitika. The various smaller and larger jewellry shops offer these articles; for example the *Hokitika Crafts Gallery* on Tancred Street or the *Westland Greenstone,* located directly opposite.

Important Addresses: Information is available from the *Public Relations Office,* corner of Tancred and Weld Street.

Police: Police Station, Sewell St., Tel: 580 88.

Post Office: corner of Revell and Weld Street.

Holidays and Celebrations

It is important to note that holidays in New Zealand will be moved to a more favourable date if they happen to fall in the middle of the week. For example, if the date falls on a Tuesday, Wednesday or Thursday, the holiday will be celebrated on the previous Monday. If it falls on the remaining days of the week, then the following Monday will be set as the date. Public holidays are: January 1 (New Year's Day), February 6 (Waitangi Day), Good Friday, Easter Monday, April 25 (Anzac Day), the first Monday in June (the Queen's Birthday), the fourth Monday in October (Labour Day), December 25 (Christmas Day) and December 26 (Boxing Day).

Regional Holidays include January 22 (Wellington), January 29 (Auckland and Northland), February 1 (Nelson), March 31 (Taranaki), March 23 (Southland and Otago), November 1 (Hawkes' Bay and Marlborough), December 1 (Westland) and December 16 (Canterbury).

Invercargill

Deep in the southern region of the South Island is the eighth largest city in New Zealand, Invercargill, with a population of approximately 54,000. The city is spaciously laid out with an abundance of parks. It was founded in 1853; today, thanks to the fertility of the surrounding land, Invercargill has become the economic centre of this region. From Invercargill, one can easily take a trip to the coastal Fjordland National Park *(→National Parks)* or visit *→Stuart Island* by airplane. The ferries depart from Port Bluff located 27 kilometres (17 miles) away. There is a city museum, *Southland Museum & Art Gallery,* which is especially interesting because of the New Zealand tuatara lizard exhibit in the terrarium.

Invercargill / **Practical Information**

Accommodation

The largest hotel in Invercargill is the *Kelvin Hotel,* Kelvin St., Tel: (3) 218 28 29 with standard prices from NZ$ 96 for singles and NZ$ 100 for doubles. On Dee Street, one will also find the *Grand Hotel,* Tel: (3) 218 80 59, with single rooms priced from NZ$ 45 and doubles from NZ$ 76.

The *Youth Hostel,* Tel: (3) 215 93 44, is located somewhat outside of the city at 122 North Road. The hostel is priced at NZ$ 11 per night.

Eight kilometres (5 miles) outside the city, but near Oreti Beach, is the *Beach Road Motor Camp,* Tel: 330-400. A tent site costs NZ$ 6.50, cottages are priced from NZ$ 12. Only one kilometre (a little over half a mile) from the centre of town is the *Invercargill Caravan Park,* Victoria Avenue, Tel: (3) 218 87 87. A tent site here costs NZ$ 5 per person.

Automobile Association: The office is located at 47 Gala Street.

Car Rental: "Avis," 109 Spay Street.

Medical Care: Southland Hospital, Kew St., Tel: (3) 218 19 49 or Dr. Hardy Hunt, 83 Don St., Tel: (3) 218 63 43.

Restaurants: Among the countless restaurants in Invercargill is *Gerard's* opposite the train station, which serves typically New Zealand cuisine. Other specialities can be found in *Ainos Steak House* on Dee Street.

Numerous pubs offer a wide selection of hot meals; for example, *Avenal Homestead,* corner of Dee and Avenal Street, where meals are inexpensive and good. *Kelvin Carvery,* on Kelvin Street, has quite an extensive menu.

Fast food and take-aways can be found everywhere in the centre of town but are especially concentrated along Dee Street.

Swimming: A visit to the warm water swimming pools either on Conon Street or Queen's Drive at the end of Queen's Park will prove quite relaxing. A beautiful beach is located around 10 kilometres (6¹/₄ miles) west of town, called Oreti.

Transportation: Airplanes trains and buses make travel to other cities quite convenient. This city also has ferry connections to →*Stuart Island.*

Important Addresses

The *Visitor Information Service* is located at 82 Dee Street.

Police: Central Police Station, Don Street, Tel: (3) 214 40 39.

Post Office: Located at the end of Dee Street.

Kaikoura

The small, sleepy town of Kaikoura is located in the northeastern portion of
the South Island, directly along the coast. Kaikoura can best be reached from
Christchurch and heading north, following along the eastern coast. This
coastline has a much different character than the western coast: the coves
and cliffs have a much gentler appearance. The Pacific Ocean does not pound
the cliffs with as much violence as does the Tasman surf on the west coast.
The city itself is famous for its crayfish, which taste similar to and as good
as lobster. Earlier, whales were hunted; today, people live from harvesting the
crayfish. One can, however, still take a tour to observe the whales off the coast
of Kaikoura. These trips are aboard a cutter and last around three hours. The
tour costs NZ$ 60.

Those who consider this too expensive, can at least take some pictures of the
seals in the colony along the coast of Kaikoura. This hike can also be extended to include the mountains surrounding Kaikoura. The countryside with the
impressive limestone caves offers a welcome change from the sooner colourless
city, whose Maori name can be linguistically traced to the term for crayfish.

Kaikoura / **Practical Information**

Accommodation: There are a few smaller hotels and motels in Kaikoura. *Blue
Seas Motel,* The Esplanade, Tel: 319 54 41, singles NZ$ 56, doubles NZ$ 62.
Oregon Court Motel, 169 Beach Road, Tel: 319 56 23, singles NZ$ 45, doubles
NZ$ 57.

The campsite *Kaikoura Holiday Camp* is located near the train station on Beach
Road, Tel: 207. It has only very few tent sites (NZ$ 5.50), but quite a lot of dif-
ferent types of cottages priced from NZ$ 11.

Restaurants: Worth mentioning first are the take-aways in this city, because
where else in the world are there snack bars serving lobsters? In Kaikoura,
these are located along the coastal road. Another local delicacy is the
"crabstick." Those who prefer a more stylish ambience can dine in the *Craypot
Restaurant.*

Kaitaia

This small town, located in Northland *(→Regions)* gains importance as a point
of departure for trips to *→Ninety Mile Beach.* Those who would like to take
a break can visit the *Far North Regional Museum.* It is located on Great South

Road and has an excellent collection of exhibits pertaining to navigation. Here, one can also see displays of taxidermically prepared animals native to New Zealand, including even the now extinct Moa bird. The museum is open weekdays from 10 am to 5 pm, weekends from 1 to 5 pm. Admission is NZ$ 2.

Kaitaia / **Practical Information**

Accommodation

Kaitaia Hotel. Commerce Street, Tel: (9) 408 03 60, singles NZ$ 45, double NZ$ 52.

Motel Capri, 5 North Road, Tel: (9) 408 02 24, singles NZ$ 51, doubles NZ$ 57.

Sierra Court Motel, North Road, Tel: (9) 408 14 60, singles NZ$ 56, doubles NZ$ 68.

There is a wide selection of numerous other hotels and motels since Kaitaia is visited by a large number of tourists.

There are also plenty of tent sites: in Kaitaia, the *Dyers Motor Camp,* 69 South Road, Tel: 39, tent sites cost NZ$ 6 per person, cottages are priced from NZ$ 20. 18 kilometres (11 1/2 miles) west of the city in Ahipara is the *Pine Tree Lodge Motor Camp,* priced at NZ$ 7. Also 18 kilometres (11 1/2 miles) away, but to the north, is the *Ninety Mile Beach Holiday Park,* with tent sites priced at NZ$ 7.

Medical Care: Kaitaia Hospital, Redan Rd., Tel: (9) 408 00 11 or Dr. Hilmer Bedelmann, 37 Puckey Ave., Tel: (9) 408 11 70.

Restaurants: There are not very many restaurants in Kaitaia, but what can be recommended is *Steve's Snapper Bar* at 123 Commerce Street. One can also dine in the *Kaitaia Hotel.* Other than these, there are a number of take-aways.

Important Addresses

Police: Kaitaia Police Station, Redan Road, Tel: (9) 408 04 00.

Kerikeri

This idyllic town on the →*Bay of Islands* is inviting for a relaxing stay. From this town it is possible to take extensive hikes through the Northland region (→*Regions*) or spend a day sunbathing on one of the secluded bays along the coast. Kerikeri is also an important region for the cultivation of citrus fruits.

Kerikeri / **History**

The Maori had already discovered the fertility of the Northland region at a relatively early stage in the development of this area. The soil in Kerikeri is also suited for growing sweet potatoes. This region is rich in numerous other mineral resources as well. With the arrival the first European settlers in 1819, the first missionary base was founded in Kerikeri.

Kerikeri / **Sights**

There are two especially interesting monuments in Kerikeri: the first mission and the oldest stone house in New Zealand. They are located adjacent to each other on the outskirts of town when heading toward Rainbow Falls across the river. The mission house was built in 1822 by John Butler. It was renamed *Kemp House* by its second owner. The Kemp family, a missionary family, then lived in this house up until 1974, when they donated it to the Historic Place Trust. This house, built in European architecture can be visited weekdays from 10:30 am to 12:30 pm and from 1:30 to 4:30 pm; admission NZ$ 2.50.

Stone Store, the oldest stone house in New Zealand also dates back to the same era. It houses a small museum open daily from 10 am to 5 pm. Another sight worth seeing is the partially restored Maori village, *Rewa's Village,* open daily from 10 am to 5 pm. It is located across the river on a mountainside. Historical times come to life in this village with its assembly hall and other Maori sites. This village leads to a better understanding of the Maori culture, customs and daily life. Paths through this village lead by plants typical to New Zealand and include informative plaques with specific botanical details.

Kerikeri / **Practical Information**

Accommodation

A sufficient number of motels can be found in and around Kerikeri, which applies to the entire Bay of Islands.

Colonial House Lodge, 178 Kerikeri Road, Tel: (9) 407 91 06, singles NZ$ 62, doubles NZ$ 64.

The cozy *Kerikeri Youth Hostel,* Tel: (9) 407 93 91, on the main street, offers accommodation for NZ$ 11. For campers, there is the *Aranga Holiday Park,* Kerikeri Road, Tel: (9) 407 93 26, offering beautiful tent sites for NZ$ 8, or one can rent a cottage for NZ$ 32. On Pa Road is an additional camping site *Pagoda*

Lodge Caravan Park, Tel: (9) 407 86 17, which is also nicely located, offering inexpensive tent sites from NZ$ 7.

Car Rental: "Avis" on Cobham Road.

Medical Care: Kerikeri Medical Services, Homestead Road, Tel: (9) 407 97 11.

Restaurants: Although this village is quite small, there are plenty of take-aways, cafés and pubs. Complete meals are available at the centrally located *Homestead Hotel.*

Important Addresses

Police: Kerikeri Police Station, Kerikeri Road, Tel: (9) 407 92 11.

Post Office: Corner of Cobham and Kerikeri Road.

Kiwi

In New Zealand, there are three things with the term "kiwi": the nocturnal bird incapable of flight, the well known fruit and the residents of New Zealand.

The "Lake of a hundred islands" — lake Manapouri

Lakes

There are so many lakes at which to marvel in →*Aotearoa* that it is virtually impossible to name all of them. Each has its own charm and beauty. A few of the most significant lakes are briefly described below to provide an overview.

Lake Grasmere

This lake is located in the northern regions of the South Island, south of the city of →*Blenheim.* Its primary importance is its salt extraction plant.

Lake Hawea

Lake Hawea is a beautiful spot in central Otago *(→Regions).* 16 kilometres (10 miles) from the town of Wanaka is this lovely lake with lush vegetation on its banks like willows and poplars. What is especially nice are hikes through the surrounding mountain regions where one will have a good view of the lake. It is also possible to fish for salmon and trout in this lake or even rent a kayak and paddle around the lake.

Lake Manapouri

Lake Manapouri is located 19 kilometres (12 miles) south of →*Te Anau,* in the impressive Fjordlands *(→National Parks).* It is known as "the lake of a hundred islands." From here, day trips to →*Doubtful Sound* are possible, but one can also to take a boat trip around the lake beginning at the town of Manapouri leading to the "Manapouri Hydroelectric Power Station." A visit to this complex allows one to observe the operation of the generator turbines. This turbine is in a tunnel 213 metres (697 feet) under the lake. From there the water is channelled through long pipes to Doubtful Sound. After having visited the power station, the trip then continues for about four hours across the lake. One can then opt for an eight hour tour of Doubtful Sound which is very much worthwhile. This tour costs NZ$ 88.

Lake Matheson

Lake Matheson is located only a few miles from the town of Fox near →*Fox Glacier.* The lake itself has numerous hiking paths leading through the forest with its diverse vegetation. The lake shimmers with colours, offering an especially beautiful view with its lush surroundings. This lake, however, is often visited for another reason: when the weather is clear, Mount Cook (elevation: 3,764 metres/12,308 feet) is reflected in the lake, making one of the most beautiful photographic motifs that one will encounter in New Zealand.

Lake Paringa

This is one of a total of eleven lakes which can be found in the general region of Haast. Lake Paringa lies directly between Haast and Hokitika and is well known for the numerous species of birds which nest on its banks. This is a wonderful place for those interested in ornithology. The rain forest in this area is also worth seeing.

Lake Rotorua

Lake Rotorua is the largest of twelve lakes near →*Rotorua*. It is a beautiful lake, well suited for hikes and tours by boat. Whether an organised boat tour to the island of Mokoia or simply a trip around Rotorua in a paddle boat, this area is definitely worth spending some time.

Lake Taupo

The largest lake in New Zealand in the heart of the North Island is, like Lake Rotorua, in a crater. At an altitude of 357 metres (1,168 feet), this lake covers an area of 606 square kilometres (234 square miles). There is quite a lot of activity at this lake during the entire year, mainly because it is located near one of the most heavily frequented tourist areas. A number of sports can be undertaken here and local residents as well as tourists do just this. In addition to the numerous aquatic sports possible, the trout in this lake make it an absolute must for fishermen.

Lake Te Anau

This is the largest lake on the South Island (53 square kilometres/ 21 square miles), located near the town of →*Te Anau* in a beautiful landscape. This area is often referred to as "the gateway to Fjordland." Extended boat trips are available to the "Glow-worm Caves" (for further information →*Te Anau).*

Lake Wakatipu

Lake Wakatipu is situated in a glacial valley with the city of →*Queenstown* along its banks. With an area of 72,500 acres it is the third largest lake in New Zealand. Here, all sorts of water sports are possible. On the northern end of Lake Wakatipu is the small settlement of Glenorchy, which is a good point of departure when exploring the *Routeburn Track (→Mount Aspiring National Park under National Parks).*

Lake Wanaka

This impressive alpine lake is on the South Island. Many who visit Lake Wanaka will find it a holiday paradise because of its diverse landscapes and innumerable opportunities for recreational activities. The small village of Wanaka has adapted to tourism. It is an important location as a base for a visit to *Mount Aspiring National Park (→National Parks)*.

Language

Although English is the official language of New Zealand, one will realise that a unique way of speaking has developed. Far more foreign sounding is the Maori language. It is taught in schools and universities but most of the Maori do speak English.

Some common New Zealand usage:

gidday!	hello, good day (as a greeting)
bloody	very
cracker	great, super (for people as well as things)
good on ya!	well done!
jersey	sweater, jumper
jug	beer mug

Lake Wakatipu is the third largest lake in New Zealand

mate	pal, buddy
paddock	pasture, open field
she'll be right	it's ok
to shout a drink	to buy a round

Maori Terms:

haere mai	welcome
haere ra	farewell
kia ora	I wish you good health
ao te aroha	the land of the great white cloud
whare	house
marae	an assembly place
pa	fortified village
haka	war dance
tapu	taboo

The Marlboro Sounds on the South Island — even today there is still an ele-ment of pristine paradise

Literature

A Tramper's Guide New Zealand's National Parks, Reed Methuen Publishers Ltd., 1987.
Collins Handguide to Native Trees of New Zealand, Collins Publisher Ltd., 1988
The bestseller by Keri Hulme is the book *The Bone People.*

Maps

The best street and city maps can be obtained through the Automobile Association. Trail maps for individual regions and for national parks are available at the NZTP offices or in local tourist information offices. These are continually updated and, what is more, make a nice souvenir. City maps are also often available free of charge.

Mahia Peninsula →*Regions: Hawkes' Bay*

Marlborough Sounds

The fascinating region of Marlborough Sounds on the South Island has remained, for the most part, a well preserved natural paradise. Countless miles of canals, beaches, secluded coves and islands make up this breathtaking countryside. The landscape is covered with what appears to be impenetrable vegetation. The Marlborough Sounds were home to the European settler Abel Tasman and Captain James Cook landed here a hundred years later to frequently return. Thanks to his detailed recount, Marlborough Sounds became the most well known area in the southern hemisphere. This region later became a docking point for the fleets of whaling ships. The Marlborough Sounds were, however, not spared from conflicts: land was scarce around the Nelson region making it necessary for settlers to push eastward. The population of the Marlborough Sounds steadily increased, much to the displeasure of the Maori tribes. Later, conflicts between the European settlers arose.
Finally, the colonial government declared the Marlborough Sounds an independent region. →*Picton,* which was at that time the settlement Waitohi, was declared capital city of this region. In 1865, the city already lost this status to the settlement which is now →*Blenheim.*

Masterton

Masterton is located near Wellington. This city is an important centre for the agricultural area of Wairarapa and the venue for the "Golden Sheers Competition," an international match for sheep sheering techniques, attracting participants from around the world. In addition, *Queen Elizabeth Park,* featuring a collection of miniature trains, and *Wairarapa Art Centre* are both worth visiting. Outside the city, one can observe the fascinating ornithological collection in the *Mount Bruce Native Bird Reserve.*

Masterton / **Practical Information**

Medical Care: Masterton Public Hospital, Te Ore Ore Road, Tel: (6) 377 20 99 or Dr. R. D. Wigley, 20 Workshop Road, Tel: (6) 378 84 88.
Important Addresses
Police: Park Avenue, Tel: (6) 378 61 66.

Maunganui

Maunganui is a small resort on the →*Bay of Plenty,* favoured by many New Zealanders as a holiday destination. It lies at the foot of Mount Maunganui with an elevation of 232 metres (759 feet). It offers a beautiful panorama of the region. The small harbour is filled with sail boats during the peak season and beautiful beaches attract avid aquatic sportsmen and sunbathers. The saltwater pools at the base of the mountain make an interesting and enjoyable bathing experience.

Maunganui / **Practical Information**

Accommodation: The *Anchor Inn Hotel,* on Maunganui St., charges NZ$ 25 per night, as does the *Oceanside Hotel* on the corner of Marine Parade and Adams Avenue.
Since the main attraction of this town are the beaches, there are a number of camping sites. The *Omanu Beach Holiday Park,* 70 Ocean Beach Road, charges NZ$ 9 per night. The *Ocean Pines Motor Camp,* Maranui Street, charges NZ$ 7.50 and the *Mount Maunganui Domain Motor Camp,* located directly at the base of the mountain charges NZ$ 6. All three of these also offer rental cottages.

Restaurants: There is not a large selection of restaurants in this town. At the *Anchor Inn Hotel* on Maunganui Street, snacks and light meals are served, as well as at *Simple Foods,* located on the same street.

Important Addresses

The *Information Centre* is located on Maunganui Road, when heading out of town toward Tauranga.

Medical Care

Those confronted with health problems in New Zealand need not worry about the medical standards. The level of education and the quality of equipment and facilities in hospitals are very good. Payment is, however, expected in advance for treatment and medication. It is, therefore, recommended that supplemental travel insurance be taken out for the duration of the trip. Most major insurance companies and even some airlines offer such policies. Travel insurance is usually quite reasonably priced and may even include travel costs for necessary treatment in one's home country resulting from injuries. These policies are usually limited to the exact dates of travel.

Often, there is a special clause relating to accidents occurring in New Zealand. The injured party will receive full compensation regardless of who is at fault.

Money

Depending on the current exchange rate, it is best to buy traveller's cheques in US dollars. These are accepted at all banks and currency exchange offices. Both are abundant in all of the cities and towns in New Zealand. Other currencies are also widely accepted. Banks are open Monday through Friday from 10 am to 4 pm; currency exchange offices will generally have longer business hours and are often open during the weekends. There is no limit to the amount of currencies that can be brought into or taken out of New Zealand. Credit cards are also widely accepted, even at some of the campsites.

Mount Egmont →*Mt. Egmont National Park under National Parks*

Napier

The city of Napier on the North Island is situated on Hawkes' Bay *(→Regions).* This is one of the most important regions for the production of wine. Of the two cities constructed in the Art Deco architecture, Napier is the more widely known and is similar to Hastings in international reputation, gaining renown from the coastal resorts. Since 1858, the city of Napier has been the provincial capital. Its countryside is characterised by numerous vineyards and it is one of the most important cities for the wool and textiles industries.

Napier / **History**

February 3, 1931 is an important day in the history of Napier. On this date, a massive earthquake shook the region and levelled the cities of Napier and Hastings, leaving nothing more than ashes and rubble. Thousands of the unemployed settled around Hawkes' Bay to assist in the reconstruction of these two cities. The architectural trend at that time was Art Deco and both of these cities were rebuilt in this style.

Napier / **Sights**

Of course the first interesting aspect of the city is its architecture. Tours around the city are also available. Unfortunately, these are only offered on Sundays. They depart from the museum at 2 pm and cost NZ$ 3.50. The river promenade, *Marine Parade,* is a beautiful place for leisurely stroll. Along this route, one can admire the magnificent parks and gardens; the promenade itself is lined with trees native to New Zealand. Located on Marine Parade is also *Marineland,* where one can see the performing seas and dolphins. Marineland is open daily from 9:30 am to 4:30 pm and costs NZ$ 4.50 admission. Another attraction is *Lilliput,* a miniature town with miniature trains and a planetarium. Somewhat further north on Marine Parade is the *Nocturnal Wildlife Centre* where one can make the acquaintance of the flightless kiwi bird. It is open 10 am to 4 pm and admission is NZ$ 2.50.

Napier / **Museums and Galleries**

At the end of Browning Street at the junction of Marine Parade is *Hawkes' Bay Art Gallery & Museum.* Here impressive pieces pertaining to the history of the region are on display as are relics from the Maori culture as well as from the era of European settlers. Especially interesting is the photo documentary on the earthquake. The museum is open weekdays from 10:30 am to 4:30 pm, weekends from 2 to 4:30 pm. Admission costs NZ$ 2.

Napier / **Practical Information**

Accommodation

Located near the beach is the *Blue Lagoon Motel,* 27 Meeanee Quay, Tel: (6) 835 96 26, singles NZ$ 58, doubles NZ$ 70, and on Hastings Street, the *Fountain,* Tel: (6) 835 73 87, singles NZ$ 56, doubles NZ$ 65.

Guest houses have also established themselves along Marine Parade; almost all of these offer accommodation including breakfast: *Waterfront Lodge,* 36 Marine Parade, Tel: (6) 835 34 29, singles NZ$ 26, doubles NZ$ 38, or *Pinehaven Private Hotel,* 42 Marine Parade, Tel: (6) 835 55 75, singles NZ$ 36, doubles NZ$ 48.

The *Napier Youth Hostel,* 47 Marine Parade, Tel: (6) 570 39, charges NZ$ 11. As is so often the case the camping sites are located outside of town; the nearest one is *Kennedy Park,* Tel: (6) 843 91 26 in Marewa. For tent sites, one will pay NZ$ 7 and for a cottage, between NZ$ 30 and NZ$ 50.

Automobile Association: The office is located on Dickens Street.

Car Rental: "Avis" at 14 Station Street.

Medical Care: Napier Hospital, Hospital Terrace, Tel: (6) 835 49 69 or Hawkes' Bay Health Services, 30 Munroc St., Tel: (6) 835 46 96.

Restaurants: A restaurant which can be recommended not only because of its Art Deco architecture is *Dijon's,* 80 Emerson Street. This restaurant offers a wide variety of excellent cuisine. Also offering good food is *Drago's Restaurant,* 14 Raffles Street, and for those who enjoy Indonesian cuisine, *Restaurant Indonesia,* 90 Marine Parade. The selection of Chinese restaurants is also quite large. Fast food restaurants and take-aways are especially concentrated along Emerson Street.

Important Addresses

The *Information Centre* on Marine Parade is open on weekdays 8:30 am to 5 pm, on weekends from 9 am to 5 pm.

Police: Napier Police Station, Station Road, Tel: (6) 835 46 88.

Post Office: Corner of Dickens and Hastings Street.

National Parks

New Zealand is, without a doubt, exceptional for its national parks. One will not only meet tourists from around the world in these parks, but residents of New Zealand as well. Each national park has its own character and kept in immaculate condition. The parks are designed so that inexperienced hikers can find their way through them as easily as more experienced naturalists. The paths and trails are laid out in differing degrees of difficulty making it possible to find a trail appropriate to one's own ability.

The following is a short summary of the twelve national parks: four are located on the North Island; eight, on the South Island.

National Parks / **North Island**

Egmont National Park

The Egmont National Park is located on the western coast of the North Island. Mount Egmont, known to date as Mount Taranaki to the Maori, towers at the centre of the park, measuring 320 square kilometres (124 square miles). Here, one will find all forms of vegetation, and always in view is the conical volcano reaching an altitude of 2,518 metres (8,234 feet). Mount Egmont is surrounded by farmland. The ash and mud from former volcanic eruptions make for excellent topsoil. The snowcapped peak is surrounded by a belt of forests. The forest is excellent for hiking. The higher one goes, the easier it is to note the changes in the alpine vegetation. Higher up, trees become more sparse and the ground is more often covered by shrubs typical of tundra regions. Even higher, only grasses grow and eventually the ground becomes bare volcanic rock. The weather in the higher region of the Egmont National Park is often harsh, but just as often, one can enjoy the sunshine. The trails range from day trips to hikes lasting several days spending the nights in cabins or even guided mountain climbing expeditions.

Practical Information

Information is available at the Visitors Centre in New Plymouth or at the Visitors Centre in Egmont National Park at the end of Egmont Road.

Wanganui National Park

A relatively young national park and relatively easy to explore, the Wanganui National Park lies east of Egmont National Park. The park was established in 1987, offering visitors a variety of landscapes including forests, rugged cliffs and the meandering Wanganui River. Those tired of walking can enjoy a portion of this national park by taking a boat trip on the Wanganui River. Canoes are one option and jet boat tours are also available.

Practical Information

Further information is available in the Wanganui Visitors Centre.

Tongariro National Park

In the heart of the North Island is Tongariro National Park, the oldest national park in the country. Volcanoes, hot springs and geysers tell the geological history of this region. One's attention is immediately drawn to the three volcanoes towering above everything else: Mount Ruapehu (2,797 metres/9,146 feet), Mount Ngauruhoe (2,291 metres/7,491 feet) and Mount Tongariro (1,968 metres/6,435 feet). The fact that Tongariro was the first national park in New Zealand and the fourth in the world is the results of the efforts of the prudent Maori Chief Te Heuheu IV, who was a member of the Tukino tribe with Ngati Tuwharetoa origin. As the Europeans settled here, they took over an increasing amount of Maori land. Te Heuheu wanted to protect this area, which his forefathers had settled as well as the volcanoes which had been declared tabu. In 1887, he gave the land to the government under the condition that it would be maintained in its original condition and protected.

The bizarre volcanic landscape with its crater lake in Tongariro National Park

This is an impressive park. The view of the three volcanoes alone is something spectacular. The diverse countryside adds to this grandeur. There is lush alpine vegetation alongside the streams; in contrast, the closer one comes to the still active volcanoes, the more the landscape is characterised by bizarre lava formations. One can spend days in this park and a number of interesting tours are offered. *Le Chateau,* the hotel and visitors centre, is the point of departure for many of the tours, for example the two hour hike to *Taranaki Falls.* The tour leads through a variety of vegetation, forest of fern trees, so-called "pongas," palms and unusual pine trees. The Taranaki Falls can be reached quickly. The Ketetahi Walk begins about 20 kilometres (13 miles) from the *Le Chateau Hotel.* This hike leads through thick forests, over natural stairways and bridges, leading up a steep incline through dark green bushes and volcanic landscapes. The higher the altitude, the more rugged the hike. However, even inexperienced hikers will be able to accomplish this hike. The *Ketetahi Springs* are sacred springs above the timber line, which still belong to the Maori. The hot water gushes up from the earth, flowing over a series of terraces and collecting in individual pools along the way. Here, one can sit in the warm water even when the air temperatures are relatively chilly. There are cabins located nearby making an early start to hike up the volcanoes possible.

Hikes leading to the volcanoes begin at the entrance to the park. The 7½ hour hike to the summit of Mount Ngauruhoe begins at the end of Mangatepopo Road, 6 kilometres (4 miles) from State Highway 47. After about an hour, one will reach the *Soda Springs,* which smell strongly of sulphur. The volcanic rock rises gradually, forming hills and mountains with fascinating shapes. The path slowly becomes steeper and more rugged. The smoke from the volcano Mount Ngauruhoe now becomes visible. Finally, one will reach the saddle between Mount Tongariro and Mount Ngauruhoe. From here, one can set out in different directions. One trail leads to Crater Lakes, another leads to Mount Tongariro. It is also possible to climb Mount Ngauruhoe. This climb involves a great deal of effort; however, it is not dangerous and definitely worthwhile. Once traversing this slippery sand path — at times on all fours — one will be rewarded with a spectacular view of the entire region. Here, one can see Crater Lake with its shimmering colours or take a look into the bubbling, steaming volcanic crater. This hike will leave an unforgettable impression.

Practical Information

Information on this national park is available at the Le Chateau Hotel as is in-depth information on tours and hikes as well as the current weather forecast. There is also a campsite and few stores.

Urewera National Park

Urewera National Park lies to the northeast of Tongariro National Park and State Highway 38 leads through it. The beauty of this park results from the diverse shades of green of the "native bush" vegetation. No matter where one looks, paths and trails lead into the pristine nature, giving the impression of being in the deepest jungle. However, one need not worry about wild animals. There is hardly any other region with such a diversity of plant life. Here, one will discover moss-covered trees, the age of which spans centuries, wild boars and a wealth of birds. The point of departure for many tours is Lake Waikaremoana, where one can also spend the night in a tent or cabin. Those who would rather not wander through this park on their own can take a guided tour lasting five days. The tour leads from Ruatoria to the banks of the Whakatane River. One can also explore the park by boat. There are a number of opportunities for hunters; however, permits are required. Since only gravel roads lead through the national park to Lake Waikaremoana, the ride is rather bumpy. There are also numerous Maori villages along the way, in which the "typical" original inhabitants of this country still live as one might imagine they had years ago.

One short and easy hike starting at the information centre is the Hinerau Track, which passes by two beautiful waterfalls, the Momahaki Falls and the Te Tangi O Hinerau Waterfalls. The Ngamoko Track is also very nice. After only fifteen minutes on this trail, one will reach a mighty rata tree. The age, height and sheer dimensions of this tree are not all that make it special, but its gigantic root system is also fascinating. The Ngamoko Track ends with a spectacular view of Lake Waikaremoana. It is also recommended to explore the Onepoto Caves. The two hour hike leads over a path through and over a number of caves.

Practical Information

The Visitors Centre is located in Aniwaniwa, a small village. The park is directly between Rotorua and Wairoa.

National Parks / **South Island**

Abel Tasman National Park

Possibly one of the most beautiful — although by New Zealand standards, one of the smaller — national parks is named after the Dutch discoverer. The park lies on the north end of the South Island, measuring about 45,000 acres in area. The fascination of Abel Tasman National Park is hard to describe since everyone experiences this park differently — not only because it can be explored on two different trails: the coastal trail and the inland trail. One can begin with the coastal trail in Kaiteriteri, about 50 kilometres (32 miles) from Nelson. Busses operate from here daily. Small boats then bring visitors to *Sandy Bay*. Only a small section of the trail is steep, otherwise it is not very strenuous. One will always be able to see the ocean through the green thicket. After three hours, one will reach the *Anchorage Hut*. The next stop after a little over an hour is *Torrent Bay;* after another three hours, *Bark Bay.* All of these offer accommodation either in cabins or in a tent one must bring along. The last leg of the hike leads to *Awaroa Bay.* Here, there is an excellent cabin along the river and a green field where one can pitch a tent. From here, one needs to wade through the ocean which is only possible during low tide. Since other hikers are few and far between, it is possible to lay claim on one of these bays as a "private" swimming area. The next stations along the coastal trail are: *Goat Bay, Totaranui, Anapai Bay, Whariwharangi Bay* and *Wainui Inlet.* Before reaching Whariwharangi Bay, it is worthwhile to take a detour to *Separation Point,* offering a view of the entire coastal region. At the Wainui Inlet, one must once again wade through the ocean to reach the village. The best way back to Nelson is via Takaka and Pohara.

Practical Information

In Nelson, whether at the Visitors Centre or at the individual motor camps, one will be able to find an abundance of information on the Abel Tasman National Park. Since the park is suited for hikes lasting several days, one should definitely purchase and "orange pass." This pass, costing NZ$ 4 per person, is required to spend the night in the park, whether in a cabin or a tent. Passes are checked by park rangers along the way or at the cabins. One should also bring along plenty of supplies since there are no stores along the way.

Paparoa National Park

A few miles south of Abel Tasman National Park, directly on the coast, is the Paparoa National Park. This is also quite a young national park — founded in 1986 — with an area of 70,000 acres. It is a fascinating wilderness with the rugged western coast reaching into the inland regions. The best known destination in Paparoa National Park are the → *Pancake Rocks* near Punakaiki. The walk to the Pancake Rocks is short and not strenuous, beginning at the Punakaiki Information Centre. After walking only five minutes through the ferns and palm trees, one will arrive at the first "blow hole," a show of nature which is not too common in the world. The ocean water is driven into these holes in the rock by the high tide and the strong winds making the water appear to shoot up like the fountains of geysers. Five minutes further, one will have a perspective of the Pancake Rocks — a fascinating rock formation that actually does look like stacks of pancakes.

Practical Information

In Punakaiki, information is available on this park including accommodations. The nearest larger city is →*Greymouth,* about 40 kilometres (25 miles) away.

In Abel Tasman National Park, secluded coves are abundant

Westland National Park

Westland National Park is located south of Paparoa National Park along the western coast in the interior of the island. This park offers a spectrum of contrasts with an abundance of trails leading through the diverse landscapes. The two glaciers →*Franz-Josef Glacier* and →*Fox Glacier* are the most famous points of interest in this national park. In addition, there are over 60 other smaller glaciers to be explored. Alpine grassland, snow fields, waterfalls, forests, rivers and lakes make up the profile of Westland National Park. However, one will also stumble upon traces of the gold rush era. In addition to the glaciers, Westland National Park is also famous for the *Copland Track*. This trail leads from Mount Cook over the southern range to Fox Glacier. Only experienced hikers or those with guides should attempt this hike. One can also enjoy this national park on a helicopter or light aircraft tour.

One of the most popular hiking trails in New Zealand — the Routeburn Track

Practical Information

Information on this park is available at the Park Visitors Centres at Franz-Josef and Fox Glaciers. They will also be able to provide information on accommodation. If staying over night in the park, one can spend the night in the cabins.

Mount Cook National Park

A few miles south of Westland National Park in the interior of the island is Mount Cook National Park. At an altitude of 3,764 metres (12,308 feet) Mount Cook makes up the focal point of this national park. Here, a number of trails can be recommended. On the road to the Mount Cook settlement called *The Hermitage,* one will pass *Lake Pukaki,* into which the Tasman River empties. If the weather is clear, one can experience the beautiful reflection of Mount Cook in the waters of Lake Pukaki. The Hermitage is located about 20 kilometres1 (2¹/₂ miles) from the base of Mount Cook. From there or from the campsite a little over a mile away, a number of trails begin like the "Hooker Valley Track" or the "Historical Walk." One will have to cross some swinging bridges which requites a good deal of confidence to cross, while experiencing a strange feeling in one's stomach when crossing the wooden boards hanging over rivers and valleys. The swinging bridges are one of the unusual features of New Zealand's national parks. One interesting peculiarity of the glacial rivers is the eerie grey colour of the water, which is not dirty, but appears icy cold. Both trails are level and relatively easy to hike, leading through the alpine landscape. Another trail is the track to *Sealy Tarns.* This is, however, very steep and strenuous, but it does offer a panorama of the entire mountain landscape. Occasionally, one will hear a distant rumbling, and with a little luck, one might even see the cause of this sound: glacial avalanches in the valley.

The trail to *Kea Point* is much easier, but the view is not as spectacular.

Of course, there are a number of tours that should only be undertaken if accompanied by an experienced guide. Westland National Park is also a paradise for skiers during the winter.

Practical Information

The Hermitage is a settlement at an altitude of 762 metres (2,492 feet) and about 20 kilometres (12¹/₂ miles) from the base of Mount Cook. Information on the park as well as on accommodation is available and one can even shop here.

Mount Aspiring National Park

Located in the lower third portion of the South Island, Mount Aspiring National Park is in the island's western interior. This extensive national park is filled with alpine countrysides and untamed nature, filling avid hikers with enthusiasm. Named after Mount Aspiring (3,035 metres/9,925 feet), this park encompasses 717,908 acres, extending between the Wakatiku and Wanaka Lakes and the Tasman Sea. Exploring the nature in Mount Aspiring National Park is made possible by the numerous trails and cabins, offering the opportunity to stay for a number of days. The park is especially popular with mountain climbers. Those who would rather not hike can enjoy a portion of this park's beauty by car. Crossing the *Haast Pass* will leave an unforgettable impression of this landscape. The Haast Pass was used by the Maori to get to the jade on the western coast. The road leads through southern beech forests and small smaller side streets lead to various waterfalls.

One of the most popular "tracks" among New Zealanders and even preferred over the "Milford Track" (→*Fjordland National Park),* is the *Routeburn Track:* it begins 18 kilometres from (11 ^{1}/$_2$ miles) the small town of Glenorchy and can be reached by bus from most of the larger cities in the region. The first 2^1/$_2$ hours are a relatively easy hike through the forests and over hanging bridges, always with a view of the partially wooded, partially snowcapped mountains. The trail then leads steeply up to *Routeburn Falls.* After another half hour, one will reach the first cabin. Continuing on a steep incline, the next station is *Harrison Sattle,* at an altitude of 1,822 metres (5,958 feet). From here, one has a spectacular view of the mountains landscape. Continuing over smaller and larger snow fields, one reaches the summit.

On the descent, the next stop is *Mackenzie Hut,* on Lake Mackenzie in a beautiful valley. Another three hours leads to the very impressive *Earland Waterfall* and then to the cabin on Lake Hawden. The lake is the perfect place to relax or — if it's not too cold — swim. Only one more hour from here is the opposite end of the Routeburn Track. This 40 kilometre (25 mile) trail is best explored on a four-day tour.

Practical Information

Information on Mount Aspiring National Park is available at the Visitors Centre in Wanaka.

Fjordland National Park

Fjordland National Park is located in the western regions of the southernmost portion of the South Island. It is one of the largest national parks in the world with an area of 3 million acres. Of course, the main attraction here are the fjords, but the mountain ranges, lakes, thick forests and rugged valleys are also impressive. *Lake Te Anau* and *Lake Manapouri (→Lakes)* are considered "the gateway to Fjordland." Fjordland National Park is also the location of the deepest lake in New Zealand, *Lake Hauroko.*

Considered "the finest walk in the world" is the *Milford Track,* which is another reason why Fjordland National Park is so heavily frequented. It is 120 kilometres (76 miles) from Te Anau to Milford Sound, a stretch which takes about three days to hike, leading through the indescribably beautiful nature. The Milford Track has meanwhile become so famous that a hike along it is often only possible after having made reservations to do so months in advance. This is to ensure that the demands placed on nature are not too extreme. It is quite common that only organised hiking tours have access to Milford Track. For the horrendous sum of NZ$ 780, the most beautiful portions of this hike are presented during a four-day tour, including lodging in the cabins along the way. Those who do not enjoy these types of organised tours have the opportunity to visit Milford Sound on a boat tour. The boat trip lasts around two hours leading by the Sound's landmark *Mitre Peak* (1,692 metres/5,533 feet), past seal colonies lounging on the cliffs, and the *Bowen Falls* as well as a number of other waterfalls and attractions.

In 1988, the *Kepler Track* was officially opened in Fjordland National Park. This trail can be conquered in around three days and portions lead along the shores of Lake Te Anau and Lake Manapouri. Other popular hiking trails in this national park are the *Hollyford Track* and the *Greenstone Track.*

Practical Information

Information and brochures are available at the Visitors Centre Lake Te Anau or directly at Milford Sound as well as at the Queenstown Park Headquarters.

Arthur's Pass National Park

In the interior of the upper portion of the South Island is Arthur's Pass National Park. A total of only five roads on the southern island connect the east and west coasts. One of these leads over Arthur's Pass, the first route used by the Maori to reach the jade reserves in the western coastal regions. During the gold rush, the road gained importance, as it made reaching the gold fields possible from the Canterbury region *(→Regions).* Arthur's Pass National Park encompasses around 250,000 acres in the southern mountainous regions. A number of deep lush valleys, canyons, cliffs, picturesque and spectacular waterfalls and the impressive fauna make this park an unforgettable experience.

Whether on a short walk or a several-day hike, Arthur's Pass National Park should definitely be included in one's travel itinerary. One will also quite definitely make the acquaintance of the Kea *(→Animals and Wildlife)* the New Zealand mountain parrot.

Practical Information

The small town of Arthur's Pass has a Visitors Centre with all the necessary information on the park; organised tours are also offered.

Nelson Lakes National Park

North of Arthur's Pass National Park in the interior of the South Island is Nelson Lakes National Park. It is dominated by *Lake Rotorua* and *Lake Rotoiti.* The surrounding mountains and the diversity of the forest and lakeshore make a visit to this park a special experience. A large portion of the natural beauty could be preserved because this park is not heavily frequented by tourists. In addition to hiking, one can also swim, and the fishing is especially good in this area.

Practical Information

The Nelson Lakes National Park Visitors Centre is located in Saint Arnaud.

Nelson

This city is the capital of the Nelson region on the South Island. It is not only renowned as a centre for tobacco and hops, but also for its apple orchards, the largest in the world. This is also the sunniest city in New Zealand and has a population of 40,000. The atmosphere of this city is enhanced by the numerous crafts like pottery, and the seemingly endless beaches.

Nelson / **History**

During the mid 16th century, the Maori tribe Ngati-tumatakokiri landed in what is now Nelson. The era of Maori settlement was characterised by conflict and warfare. When the "New Zealand Company" founded Nelson as their second settlement in 1842, hardly any Maori inhabitants remained. With the steady growth of Nelson's economy, the government considered moving the capital to this city, until the conclusive decision was made in favour of Wellington.

Nelson / **Sights**

Standing out on any stroll through the city is the *Christ Church Cathedral,* surrounded by gardens. Also worth seeing on a walk through the city are the beautiful gardens in the "sunny" city: *Queen's Gardens* and the *Botanical Gardens.* Nelson is also a popular base for tours to Abel Tasman National Park (→*National Parks*) as well as for relaxing along the beautiful beaches.

Nelson / **Museums and Galleries**

In Isle Park is the *Nelson Provincial Museum,* with exhibits and photographs pertaining to the early Maori history as well as on the history of the Nelson region (→*Regions*) in general. The museum is open from Tuesday to Friday from 10 am to 4pm and 2 to 5 pm during weekends. With a spectrum of works by local artists, the *Suter Art Gallery,* Bridge Street is next to the gate to Queen's Garden. It is open from 10:30 am to 4 pm, admission is NZ$ 1.50. In the gallery, there are also occasional theatre and dance performances as well as concerts. The *South Street Gallery,* near the cathedral on Nile Street West, is a good destination for those interested in pottery. More information on the numerous other pottery workshops in Nelson is in the guide published by the Nelson Potters Association.

Nelson / **Practical Information**
Accommodation

A hotel in the upper category is *Hotel Nelson,* Trafalgar Street, Tel: (3) 548 22 99, singles and doubles from NZ$ 124. Less expensive but just as nice is the *Leisure Lodge Hotel,* 40 Waimea Road, Tel: (3) 548 20 89, with single rooms priced at NZ$ 60 and doubles at NZ$ 66. The *Alpha Inn,* 25 Muritai Street, Tel: (3) 548 60 77, charges NZ$ 28 for singles and NZ$ 56 for doubles. Near the centre of town, the *AA Motor Lodge,* Ajax Avenue, Tel: (3) 548 82 14, charges NZ$ 78 for singles and doubles.

There are an abundance of guest houses, the prices of which also include breakfast, for example *Tahuna Beach Holiday Park,* Beach Road, Tel: (3) 548 51 59, singles and doubles priced from NZ$ 33. *Abbey Lodge,* 84 Grove Street, Tel: (3) 548 88 16, charges NZ$ 51 for singles and doubles. *Palm Grove,* at 52 Cambria Street, Tel: (3) 548 46 45, singles for NZ$ 27, doubles for NZ$ 54. The *Nelson Youth Hostel,* Tel: (3) 548 88 17, is located at 42 Weka St. and charges NZ$ 11 per night. Another accommodation worth recommending is *Pavlova Farmhouse,* Tel: (3) 548 99 06, located three kilometres (2 miles) from the centre of town at 328 Brooke Street. Guests are greeted with a large portion of the sweet New Zealand speciality "pavlova," charging NZ$ 12 per night.

Automobile Association: The office is located on Halifax Street.

Car Rental: "Hardy Cars," 17 Shelbourne Street, often has inexpensive offers. Another alternative is "Avis," 143 Trafalgar Street.

Entertainment: There are two good discotheques in Nelson: in Stoke, the *Turf Hotel,* and in Tahunanui the *Lodge Hotel.* Also, many have live music occasionally.

Medical Care: Nelson Hospital, Tipahi Street, Tel: (3) 546 18 00 or Dr. Elisabeth Bostock, 60 Waimea Road, Tel: (3) 548 80 05.

Restaurants: A very good restaurant with a diverse selection on the menu is *Chez Eelco,* at 296 Trafalgar Street. This is a good place to enjoy a hot meal or simply coffee and cake. The *Colonial Restaurant,* 114 Bridge Street, serves excellent Mexican food and *Hitching Post* serves good pizza.

Swimming: Five kilometres (a little over 3 miles) from the centre of town, Tahuna Beach is best suited for swimming.

Important Addresses: Information is available at the *Public Relations Office,* on the corner of Halifax and Trafalgar Street, open weekdays from 8:30 am to 5 pm.

New Plymouth

New Plymouth is an agricultural city and the economic centre of the Taranaki region *(→Regions).* It is located on the western coast of the North Island. Still, New Plymouth is not a hectic city and its diverse vegetation gives it a special atmosphere.

New Plymouth / **History**

Before the first European immigrants settled into this region, the Maori inhabited this land having occasional tribal conflicts. The displeasure of the settlers grew shortly after their arrival in 1841 since they planned to develop the region agriculturally and needed more land to do this. Violent conflicts resulted, as the Maori tribes were not willing to give up their land. Warfare broke out in 1860 and would only come to an end with the surrender of the Maoris. New Plymouth was then free to become the economic centre of the region.

New Plymouth / **Sights**

A tour around the city will make visitors acquainted with the historical buildings and beautiful parks. Among these are the *St. Mary's Church* built in 1846 and

located on Vivian Street or *The Gables* on Brooklands Park Road, a hospital
built in 1848. The clock tower on the corner of Queen and Devon Street is,
however, much younger, constructed in 1985. Other sights worth seeing are
the *Pukekura Park,* situated on the outskirts of the city and the *Brookland Park.*
Lush vegetation, exotic flowers and small lakes give the park a unique atmosphere. There is a natural amphitheatre in the Brookland Park as well. Not
far from the city centre is the *Pukeiti Rhododendron Trust,* covering 900 acres.
The park also serves as a bird sanctuary.

New Plymouth / **Museums and Galleries**

The *Taranaki Museum* is located on the corner of Brougham and King Street.
The museum contains many exhibits pertaining to the Maori culture and the
early settlement of the region.

The *Govett-Brewster Art Gallery* on Queen Street has many pieces on New
Zealand, the Pacific islands and other cultures. The museum is open daily
from 10:30 am to 5:30 pm.

Definitely worth seeing is the *Arts and Crafts Centre* on Centennial Drive, open
from 8 am to 4:30 pm daily.

New Plymouth / **Practical Information**
Accommodation

The *Tasman Hotel,* offers very nice accommodation, located at the 140 Saint
Aubyn Street, Tel: (6) 753 61 29. A double room costs NZ$ 39 and a single
costs NZ$ 25. *Plymouth Sun Hotel,* on the corner of Leach and Hobson Street,
Tel: (6) 758 05 89, singles NZ$ 97, doubles NZ$ 105. The hotel *Princes Tourist
Court,* 29 Princes Street, Tel: (6) 758 25 66, costs NZ$ 45 for doubles and
singles. A recommended guest house is the *Aotea Private Hotel,* 26 Weymouth
St., Tel: (6) 758 24 38, singles NZ$ 32 doubles NZ$ 67.

The *New Plymouth Youth Hostel,* can be found at 12 Clawton St., costing NZ$ 11.
Camping sites like the *Aaron Court Caravan Park,* Tel: (6) 753 40 12, are located
somewhat outside the city. A tent site costs NZ$ 5 per person and a cottage,
between NZ$ 28 and NZ$ 48. There are also two possibilities in Fitzroy, about
4 kilometres (2¹/₂ miles) outside the city: the *Marantha Holiday Park,* 29 Princes
St., Tel: (6) 758 25 66, tent sites priced at NZ$ 6.50 and cottages priced from
NZ$ 32; the *Fitzroy Camp,* Beach Street, Tel: (6) 758 28 70, offers tent

sites for NZ$ 5.50 per person. The *Belt Road Camp* is located about one mile from the centre of the city, Tel: (6) 758 02 28, tent sites start at NZ$ 5.50 per person.

Automobile Association: Powderham Street.

Beaches and Swimming: The Fitzroy Beach lies about four kilometres (2¹/₂ kilometres outside the city.

Car Rental: The "Avis" office is located at 25 Liardet Street.

Entertainment: Most of the larger hotels offer entertainment programmes.

Medical Care: Taranaki Base Hospital, David St., Tel: (6) 753 61 39, or Dr. Ian Griffiths, 72 Vivian St., Tel: (6) 758 08 63.

Restaurants: In the *Bellissimo,* 38 Currie St., one will be able to enjoy Italian cuisine at affordable prices. The *Black Olive* restaurant, on Egmont Street, offers a large selection. For Chinese cuisine, one should try *Tong Restaurant,* 39 Devon Street West. Many pubs and fast food restaurants offer quick meals.

Important Addresses In the *Public Relations Office,* located on Liardet St.,

A monument to "Opo" in Opononi — the dolphin that won the hearts of the villagers

there is an abundance of information on the entire region. The office is open Monday to Friday from 8:30 am to 5pm.

Police: Central New Plymouth Station, Powderham St., Tel: (6) 757 54 49.

Post Office: Corner of Currie and Ariki Street.

Ninety Mile Beach

Ninety Mile Beach is located in the Northland region *(→Regions)*. Whoever gave the beach its name fibbed a little — it is actually only 64 miles long. The beach extends from the upper portion of the North Island at Cape Reinga to the small village of Ahipara.

According to the Maori legend, Cape Reinga has taken on special significance. It is said that after the souls of the dead travel across the land from this location to the place of their ancestry, Hawaiki.

The beauty of the seemingly endless Ninety Mile Beach is breathtaking: the fine sand, the motion of the waves and the cormorant birds which nest along the coast. Bus tours along the beach are available daily. One can either embark on the tour beginning in Ahipara or from Kaitaia (information and reservations in the information centre) or on the Bay of Islands. A day-long tour costs between NZ$ 28 and NZ$ 38.

Those who would like to sunbathe on the Ninety Mile Beach will need to bring plenty of supplies and time.

Ohakune

Ohakune is a small, sleepy town which makes a good base point for excursions into the Tongariro National Park *(→National Parks)*. During the winter months, Ohakune awakens from its period of hibernation: winter sports enthusiasts flock here and soon the streets are filled with activity.

Ohakune / **Practical Information**

Accommodation

There are many hotels and other types of accommodation available in Ohakune. However, the hotels fill up quickly in the winter and are somewhat more expensive than during the summer months. Two possibilities are the *Alpine Motel,* Miro St., Tel: (6) 358 87 58, a single or double room costs NZ$ 57 and *The Hobbit Motel Lodge,* on the corner of Goldfinch and Wye Street, Tel: (6) 358 82 48. A single room is priced from NZ$ 60 and double rooms, from NZ$ 70. For NZ$ 11, one can spend the night in the *Ohakune Youth Hostel* on Clyde St., Tel: (6) 358 87 24.

Those who would rather camp will pay NZ$ 6 per person at the *Ohakune Borough Camp,* on Moore St., Tel: (6) 358 85 61.

Restaurants: In the Ohakune Hotel on Clyde Street, is the *Griddlestone Restaurant,* offering good meals. On the same street is the *Café Stua,* the *Swiss Grischuna Restaurant* and the *Lovin' Spoonful Restaurant.*

A very good restaurant and a good value for the money is *Parklands* on Burns Street.

Important Addresses: The *Information Centre* is located on Moore Street and also has excellent information on Tongariro National Park.

Post Office: On the corner of Clyde and Rata Street.

Opononi

The tiny village of Opononi in Northland *(→Regions)* has little significance for tourists. However, a sad event took place here not too long ago. In the summer of 1955, a dolphin came to the beach of Opononi. This dolphin returned on a regular basis to be befriended by the inhabitants of the village, especially the children. The children played and swam with the dolphin, which came to be known as Opo, and soon became a part of the daily life in Opono021 Shortly before a law was passed to protect the dolphin, Opo was killed. To this day, the ''murder'' remains a mystery. A statue erected over Opo's grave keeps the memory of this dolphin alive.

Opua

Opua is a sleepy little village situated on the →*Bay of Islands.* It is an ideal location for those who enjoy sailing. In 1874, Opua established itself as an important export harbour. In this harbour today are all types of sailboats, private yachts and tour boats, offering visitors tours around the Bay of Islands. Ferries depart every 15 minutes from Opua to →*Russell,* the first capital of New Zealand.

Those who have not yet had their fill of hiking can explore many beautiful areas of Opua Forest. Here, one can hike through the pristine forest for hours, never losing sight of the ocean.

Orakei Korako

Between the main road from →*Hamilton* and →*Rotorua* is one of the nicest geothermal regions of New Zealand, Orakei Korako. Although the area is relatively heavily frequented by tourists, a large proportion of the natural setting has been preserved. On the opposite side of Lake Ohakuri, which can be crossed by small boat or kayak, are the thermal springs. The springs are especially well known for their sinter terraces (sinter is a mineral deposited by flowing water). Here, the impressive colouration can be admired. Seaweed, shadows and shades of colour seem to dance in the bubbling water. Especially fascinating is the 40 metre (130 foot) long sinter terrace, the *Great Golden Fleece.* An informational brochure, admission and the boat trip cost NZ\$ 6. Here, one can also visit the small, jade-green shimmering pond located within *Aladdin's Cave,* where Maori beauties once admired their reflections. The warm water also acts as a natural silver polish, restoring the lustre to silver jewellry.

Paihia

In this small but important city on the →*Bay of Islands,* there are few sights to see. However, the beautiful hotels and outstanding fish restaurants make

One of the most impressive geothermal areas in New Zealand — the steaming earth in Orakei Korako

this city worth visiting. The most important factor for tourists is that Paihia serves as a point of departure for many of the boat excursions around the Bay of Islands. The city was founded in 1823 as European missionary station. Paihia is also a popular city for swimming, surfing, fishing and sailing. Those who only have a short time to spend on the Bay of Islands should not miss the opportunity to take the "cream trip" offered by the Fuller agency. At one time the boats now used on the cream trip were used to collect and transport the dairy products produced on the numerous scattered farms in the Bay Islands and to bring the residents their mail and other necessary supplies. Since most of the islands are uninhabited today, this boat route has become more a tourist attraction. The cream trip departs daily at 10 am. It lasts about five hours and costs NZ$ 38.

Paihia / **Practical Information**

Medical Care: Dr. H. Tangoroa, Williams Road, Tel: (9) 402 71 32.
Important Addresses: *Police:* Paihia Community Constable, Tel: (9) 402 71 30.

The Pancakes Rocks do indeed look like stacks of pancakes

Palmerston North

Palmerston North is a pretty little university town with many parks and good shopping. The city is surrounded by farmland. The university has several leading institutes in the area of agricultural research. Other sights include the *Manawatu Museum,* the *Manawatu Art Gallery,* and the *Rugby Museum,* dedicated in its entirety to New Zealand's national sport.

Palmerston North / **Practical Information**

Accommodation

The *Coachman Hotel,* located at 134 Fitzherbert Ave., Tel: (6) 356 50 65 is a distinguished hotel. Singles and doubles cost NZ$ 124 per night. The *Awapuni Hotel* on Pioneer Highway, Tel: (6) 358 51 81, costs NZ$ 59 for a single, and NZ$ 63 for a double room. The *McKenzie Lodge,* 101 Milson Line, Tel: (6) 356 90 90, charges NZ$ 68 for singles and NZ$ 79 for doubles. Somewhat less expensive accommodation can be found in the guest house *Chaytor House Travel Hotel,* 18 Chaytor St., Tel: (6) 358 68 79, single NZ$ 38, doubles NZ$ 66. The camping site *Municipal Camp* on Dittmer Dr., Tel: (6) 358 03 49, costs NZ$ 7.

Car Rental: "Avis" is located at 21 Grey Street.

Medical Care: Palmerston North Hospital, 50 Ruahine St., Tel: (6) 356 91 69 or Albert Street Medical Centre, 171 Albert St., (6) 356 90 61.

Restaurants: The best restaurant in town is the *Déjeuner Café* located at 159 Broadway Avenue. The restaurant offers a wide selection of vegetarian dishes. In addition, there are a large number of pubs and take-away restaurants.

Important Addresses

Information is available at the *Public Relations Office,* on The Square, open Mondays to Fridays 8:30 am to 4:30 pm, Saturdays 9:30 am to 1 pm. *Police:* Central Police Station, Church Street, Tel: (6) 357 08 59.

Pancake Rocks

The Pancake Rocks are a geological formation which is definitely worth seeing. They are located about 40 kilometres (25 miles) from →*Greymouth* in Punakaiki. The unique formations actually look like stacked pancakes. The rock formations located amid a beautiful coastal landscape are the result of erosion and the constant pounding of the Tasman surf (→*Geography*). During high tide, one will be able to observe the seawater rush into the *blow holes* and shoot back out like a fountain. It is only a short walk out to the Pancake Rocks, but the view is so magnificent that most visitors will take more time to watch this curious show of nature. Those who have not had their fill of pancakes can take a seat in the adjacent café and fill up on real pancakes; this is, however, by no means inexpensive.

The People of New Zealand

The populace of New Zealand is characterised by a cultural mix, the largest proportion being the 3.3 million "pakehas," as the Maori call the New Zealanders of European descent.

Although quite cosmopolitan in their outlook, the New Zealanders' pride in their country becomes apparent in conversations with the residents.

Coming into contact with the Maori is not very easy. Although there are rarely signs of hostility or resentment felt toward other ethnic groups, a certain distance is maintained. While many of the pakehas are quite successful, the Maori often live modestly and secluded, preferably amongst their own kind. What is so fascinating about these people is their warmth, willingness to help, love of the land and closeness to nature. In many of the Maori groups, one does notice traces of resignation because their social status is often not comparable to that of the pakehas. The problem of unemployment among this segment of the population should also not be underestimated.

Nevertheless, the mixture of cultures is characterised by a peaceful coexistence. Free time is of utmost importance to the citizens of New Zealand. Sport, recreation and travel — especially within their own country — are given a high priority.

Photography

One should definitely bring photographic supplies along. This, not because the materials are in short supply, but because they are considerably more expensive, and tourists are allowed to bring only ten rolls of film per person into New Zealand.

Picton

The second city of the →*Marlborough Sounds* is Picton, directly on the Queen Charlotte Sound. Picton is a small but very lively city, visited by many travellers to New Zealand. The ferry that connects the two main islands of →Aotearoa arrives and departs from here several times daily.

Picton / **Sights**

Those who have some time to spend in Picton should visit the *Picton Museum* on London Quay. The museum is not large, but it does offer a great deal of information on the era of whaling. The museum is open daily from 10 am to 4 pm and admission costs NZ$ 1.

Between the museum and the ferry port one will see the huge shipwreck of the "Edwin Fox." The ship ran aground in Picton in 1879, and for some time, attempts have been made to restore the ship as a tourist attraction.

Picton / **Practical Information**

Accommodation

The *DB Terminus Hotel* is located centrally on High Street, Tel: (3) 573 64 52, singles NZ$ 36, doubles NZ$ 57. Also located in the centre of town is the *Picton Whalers Inn* on Waikawa Road, Tel: (3) 573 70 02, singles NZ$ 71, doubles NZ$ 87. Another good option is the *Bell Bird Motel,* Tel: (3) 573 69 12, about one kilometre (a little over ¹/₂ mile) from the downtown area, at 96 Waikawa Road. Singles and doubles cost NZ$ 37. Also located on Waikawa Road is the *Admiral's Lodge,* Tel: (3) 573 65 90; a single room costs NZ$ 45, a double, NZ$ 72.

There are a number of camping sites in and around Picton. The closest to the downtown area is the *Blue Anchor Holiday Park,* Waikawa Bay Road, Tel: (3) 573 72 12, a tent site costs NZ$ 8 per person. The next closest site is *Alexander's Motor Park* on Canterbury St., Tel: (3) 573 63 78. A tent site costs NZ$ 6 per person. Three kilometres (2 miles) outside of town on Beach Road is the *Parklands Marina Holiday Village,* Tel: (3) 573 63 43. Tent sites are priced from NZ$ 7.50. Less expensive is the *Momorangi Bay Motor Camp* 13 kilometres (8 miles) outside of Picton on Queen Charlotte Drive, Tel: (3) 573 78 95. A tent site costs NZ$ 5.

Car Rental: "Avis" Picton Ferry Terminal and 101 High Street.

Medical Care: Broadway Medical Centre, 21 Broadway, Tel: (3) 573 64 05.

Restaurants: The most expensive restaurant in the city is the *5th Bank,* Wellington Street. In addition, the pubs on London Quay offer very good meals. Here, one can choose between the *Oxley Hotel,* the *Federal Hotel* and the

Terminus Hotel. Fast food is available everywhere, and good sandwiches can be had at *The Sandwich Maker* on High Street.

Transportation: In addition to the ferry to the North Island, there are other travel options to destinations on the South Island. Directly next to the ferry terminal is the bus terminal. There are bus routes to Blenheim, Nelson and Christchurch. There are also daily train connections to Christchurch.

Important Addresses

The *Picton Information Centre* offers information not only on the city, but covering the entire Marlborough Sounds region. The information centre is located at the parking area between the ferry terminal and London Quay. It is open weekdays from 9:30 am to 4 pm and during weekends from 10 am to 3 pm.

Police: Police Station, 26 Broadway, Tel: (3) 573 64 39.

Post Office: Located directly on the harbour on Wellington Street.

Police →*Emergency*

Despite historical conflicts, peaceful coexistence marks the relationship between the "pakehas" and the Maori

Politics

New Zealand is an independent parliamentary monarchy in the British Commonwealth; therefore, the head of state is the Queen of England. She is represented in New Zealand by a Governor General, who is elected every five years. The House of Representatives has 95 members, including Maori representatives since 1867. An especially interesting milestone in the politics of New Zealand came in 1893 when it became the first country to grant women the right to vote. The voting age is 18 and parliamentary elections are held every three years. The government is currently headed by the Labour Party and the role of the opposition is in the hands of the National Party (a conservative party).

Postal Service

Post offices can be found in all of the larger cities and towns. In smaller towns and village are often housed in the "dairies" or other small general stores. Post offices are usualy open Monday to Thursday from 8 am until 5 pm, Fridays from 8:30 am until 8 pm. Telephone calls can also be placed from post offices (→ Telephone).

It is possible to have mail sent to New Zealand by general delivery. Letters should be addressed as follows: name, c/o Central Post Office, Town (without a postal code), New Zealand. These are held for one month and then usually returned to the sender.

Letters and postcards take seven to ten days to reach international destinations and costs NZ$ 1.30 (for up top ten grams). Aerogrammes cost 85 cents.

Queenstown

Those who want to lose themselves in the bustle of tourism will find Queenstown just right. In addition to the active night life, this city offers a varieties of other diversions to add variety to a visit to New Zealand. The surrounding regions are ideal for a number of excursions. The countryside alone makes touring around the area worth the time. Queenstown also offers facilities for a number of sports and recreational activities: water skiing, jet boating, horseback riding, golf, hiking and hang gliding.

Queenstown / **History**

Although it is clear that the area was settled much earlier by the Maori, the European settlers who came to Queenstown in 1855 found very few of the original inhabitants. The European settlers were primarily sheep ranchers, who quickly laid claim to the region. However, seven years later, the rustic, peaceful existence of the ranchers would come to an end with the discovery of gold on Shotover River. Once the gold supply was exhausted, the masses moved on, the sheep ranchers remained.

Queenstown / **Sights**

Queenstown is clearly laid out, making it ideal for exploring the city on foot. The pedestrian zone (The Mall) is lined with souvenir shops, jewellry stores, cafés and ice cream parlours. Those who would like to enjoy the "remarkable" panorama of the city and surrounding regions including the mountain range *The Remarkables* should take the *gondola* to Bob's Peak at an elevation of 400 metres (1,308 feet) above the city. The café/restaurant near the summit is also accessible on foot. The path to the summit leads through forests and is really not that strenuous. From the café the path leads farther to the summit. Attractions within the city of Queenstown include, for example, a visit to the *Kiwi & Birdlife Park,* located next to the gondola station. Here, one will be able to see a number of birds including the kiwi in its nocturnal house and the Kea, typical to New Zealand. The park is open daily from 9 am to 5 pm and admission costs NZ$ 4.50.

For NZ$ 3.50, one can visit *Waterworld* at Lake Wakatipu. Open 9 am to 5:30 pm daily.

Those interested in the historically based economy should not miss visiting a sheep ranch in Queenstown. It is best to combine this excursion with a trip aboard the steam ship "Earnslaw" on Lake Wakatipu. Transportation aboard this ship to *Mount Nicholas Sheep Station* costs NZ$ 28. Shorter tours not including a visit to the Sheep Station are also offered aboard the "Earnslaw." A bus tour through *Skippers Canyon* (NZ$ 40) is also recommended. Those who would prefer to try their hand at an exciting aquatic sport should try the New Zealand passion of jet boating or should take a raft trip. Most popular are trips on the Shotover River. It best to make one's way up the river at one's own pace in a jet boat and then return down the river, taking a raft trip. Since there are so many promoters in Queenstown, competition is stiff, making price comparisons worthwhile. Prices range from NZ$ 25 and NZ$ 120 depending on the length and type of trip.

23 kilometres (14^1/$_2$ miles) outside of Queenstown, *bungy jumping* is offered. Jumps can be made from *Historical Bridge* near Kawarau, head first into the river below, with one's feet fastened to a stable elastic rope. Jumps are calculated according to individual wishes depending on how far, if at all, one wants to be submerged in the river. Insane? Possibly, but loved by tourists and New Zealanders alike. Prices are about NZ$ 80 including a certificate and a T-shirt with a bungy-jumper emblem.

Another popular excursion is to →*Arrowtown,* the pretty gold mining town.

Queenstown / **Museums and Galleries**

For car enthusiasts: the *Motor Museum* at the Skyline Gondola Station has a large number of old timers and other automobiles on exhibit. It is open daily from 9 am unto 5:30 pm; admission, NZ$ 4.

Queenstown / **Practical Information**

Accommodation

Since Queenstown is a tourist destination during the entire year, there is a large number of hotels, motels and other accommodation. To name a few: *Holiday Inn Queenstown,* Queenstown St., singles NZ$ 163, doubles NZ$ 168 *Pacific Park,* Frankton Rd., Tel: (3) 442 35 40, singles and doubles NZ$ 72 *Contiki Lodge,* Sainsbury Rd., Tel: (3) 442 71 07, singles NZ$ 28, doubles NZ$ 50 An example of one of the many guest houses is *Goldfields Guest House,* 41 Frankton Rd., Tel: (3) 442 72 11. Here a room including breakfast is priced at NZ$ 51 for a single, NZ$ 72 for a double room. The *Queenstown House* 69 Hallenstein St., Tel: (3) 442 90 43 costs NZ$ 42 for a single and NZ$ 62 for a double.

The *Queenstown Youth Hostel* costs NZ$ 14 per night and is located at 80 Lake Esplanade, Tel: (3) 442 84 13.

The nearest camping site is the *Queenstown Motor Park,* Tel: (3) 442 72 54 Tent sites are priced from NZ$ 6.50, cabins from NZ$ 20 per person. Othe

---

A fantastic panorama of Queenstown and the Remarkables ▶

possibilities are the *Mountain View Lodge Holiday Camp,* Frankton Rd., Tel: (3) 442 82 46, with tent sites for NZ$ 5 per person. Six kilometres (4 miles) outside of town is the *Frankton Motor Camp,* Tel: 27-247, tent sites priced from NZ$ 7.

Entertainment: On the programme of a number of pubs in Queenstown mall, there is live music and other shows. *Eichhard's,* in the mall toward the lake, is very well frequented with various styles of music and a discotheque. On Shotover Street, one will find the *Harlequin Night Club* and there is also often live entertainment in *O'Connell's Hotel.*

Medical Care: Lakes District Hospital, Douglas St., Tel: (3) 442 30 53 or Queenstown Medical Centre, 5 Shotover St., Tel: (3) 442 73 02.

Restaurants: In addition to the *Skyline Restaurant* on Bob's Peak are *Upstairs Downstairs* or *Roaring Meg's.* Both can be found on Shotover Street. For dinners in the *Westy's Restaurant* in Queenstown Mall, one must count on paying about NZ$ 30. For less expensive Mexican food, try *Saguaro,* also in the Queenstown Mall. *The Cow,* located on Cow Lane, has excellent Italian cuisine and a very nice atmosphere. Many pubs cafés and snack bars can be found at the mall and along Shotover Street.

Transportation: All of the larger cities in New Zealand can be reached from Queenstown either by airplane or bus. The "Magic Bus" brings tourists from Queenstown to various points of interest, for instance the Routeburn Track *(→Mt. Aspiring National Park under National Parks).*

Important Addresses

The *NZTP Office* is located at 49 Shotover Street and open daily from 8:30 am to 5:30 pm. Information about the region is also available in the *Lands and Surveys Information Centre,* at the corner of Ballarat and Stanley Street, open Monday to Friday from 8 am to 5 pm. During peak season, daily.

Police: Police Station, 11 Camp Street, Tel: (3) 442 79 00.

Post Office: Located on the corner of Queenstown Mall and Camp Street.

Regions

This entry will provide the reader with an overview of the various regions into which New Zealand was once divided. The regional subdivision no longer has any political significance; however, these unofficial borders have been maintained — psychologically, at least.

Regions / **North Island**

Northland

The centre of this region is the city of →*Whangarei*. Attractions in this region are the →*Bay of Islands* and the →*Ninety Mile Beach*. The landscape of Northland is characterised by a alternating coastline. The raw climate of the northern most point of the region where the Pacific Ocean meets the Tasman Sea stands in contrast to the tranquillity of the numerous bays along the coast.

The other portion of Northland is characterised by the presence of the Kauri (→*Waipoua Kauri Forest)*. This is the last remaining forest with trees of this kind. The forest is perfect for long hikes in the shadows of these ancient trees. Two hundred years ago, Northland (which has many places of historical importance) was covered with Kauri trees. However, during the past century, the trees were cut down by European settlers hoping for large profits for this valuable wood. This land has since been made into pastureland.

Central Auckland

This region has gained in significance through the city of →*Auckland*. The largest harbour in New Zealand fuels the economic importance of the city and the region. Auckland is known for its high proportion of Polynesian residents, which gives the city a South Pacific flair.

South Auckland

South Auckland is not only the largest region of the North Island but also the most colourful. The most important city in this region is →*Hamilton*. The main attractions of South Auckland are the →*Bay of Plenty,* the →*Coromandel Peninsula,* the area around →*Rotorua* and the →*Urewera National Park.* The pristine nature with rugged coastline, gentle beaches and active geothermal areas provide a cross-section of the diverse facets of nature in New Zealand.

East Coast

The largest city of the region is →*Gisborne*. This region does not have a large diversity of landscapes. Its significance lies in the cultivation of fruit as well as the fishing industry. There is little in the way of tourist activity.

Hawkes' Bay

The city of →*Napier* is situated in the heart of this region. Hawkes' Bay is the region's most important in the cultivation of fruit, including grapes for making

New Zealand's excellent wines. The →*Mahia Peninsula* is located in this region on the road from →*Gisborne* to →*Napier.* The Peninsula's beautiful bay is excellent for scuba diving and fishing.

Wellington

This region is characterised by the Tongariro National Park *(→ National Parks)* a wonder of nature and →*Wellington,* the capital of New Zealand and an urban counterpart to this rural area. In this region, one is able to experience fascinating facets of nature as well as the flair of a big city.

Taranaki

The landscape of this region is dominated by extensive tracts of pastureland. It is named after Mount Taranaki, usually called Mount Egmont today *(→National Parks).* The most important city in this region is →*New Plymouth.* Taranaki is the centre for energy in New Zealand: extensive deposits of natural gas are found inland as well as off the coast.

Regions / **South Island**

Marlborough

Here, the regions of the South Island will be covered clockwise beginning in the northeast with the Marlborough region. The most important city on the South Island is →*Blenheim.* The region is most renowned for the →*Marlborough Sounds* with the fantastic beaches, coves and the peninsulas. The most important branches of this region's economy are fishing and the production of wine.

Canterbury

Christchurch is the capital of this region, characterised by acres and acres of farmland. Wherever one looks, one will see areas which will bring the English countryside to mind. Offering a contrast to this pastoral landscape are the mountainous regions of Canterbury. Within relatively short distances, one will experience very different landscapes — once again the diversity of New Zealand becomes apparent.

Otago

Otago stretches along the lower third of the South Island. The most important city in this region is →*Dunedin.* The central portions of Otago is used predominantly in agriculture, punctuated with hills and mountains. The main attractions are →*Queenstown, Milford Sound and Milford Track (→Fjordland National Park under National Parks)* as well as Routeburn Track *(→Mount Aspiring National Park under National Parks).* Another point of interest is the city of Oamaru, the provincial capital of the northern Otago region, situated near an extinct volcano. The core of this city is very old and it is interesting to see the housed built from the famous Oamaru limestone. In the surrounding regions, one can still find Maori cliff drawings.

One can also visit the nearby fishing village of Moeraki, which is fascinating because of a unique geological formation: a walk along the beach will lead to the *Moeraki Boulders,* huge spherical stones with a circumference of up to four metres (13 feet) and a weight of several tons.

A visit to the Otago peninsula known for its albatross colony. in addition to these interesting birds, one can also observe the penguins.

Southland

This region is at the southern tip of the South Island extending up the western coast. The largest national park in the world, the *Fjordland National Park (→National Parks)* takes up a large portion of this region. The most significant city of Southland is →*Invercargill,* which is mainly an agricultural centre.

Westland

Moving further northwards along the western cost is →*Greymouth,* the most important city in Westland. At one time, this was the centre for gold prospecting activity and lumberjacks. Today, in this region of coastline and forests, one can still experience the untamed and unexpected — a number of artists and individualists have settled here. An increasing number of local residents as well as tourists are drawn to this area because of the two national parks in this region: *Mount Aspiring* and *Westland National Parks (→National Parks).*

Nelson

The regional tour of the South Island comes to its completion with the region of Nelson, which is considered the capital *(→Nelson).* This region is especially well known for its mild climate and little rain throughout the year — two of the important reasons for the cultivation of fruit in this area. This coupled with the multitude of beaches attracts visitors from near and far. The *Able Tasman* and the *Nelson National Parks (→National Parks)* are especially popular attractions in this region.

Religion

About 26% of the population belong to the Anglican Church, 17% are Presbyterian, 14% are Catholic, 5% Methodist, 2% Baptist and about 1% still belong to the Maori Church.

Rotorua

Rotorua is to the North Island what →*Queenstown* is to the South Island. Not Rotorua itself, but the geothermal areas around the city attract masses of visitors. The hot springs, formidable geysers and mud-pots surrounded by steaming soil are what makes this city of about 51,000 so fascinating. This city is also a good place to come into contact with the Maori culture since a large number of them live here.

Rotorua / **History**

In the middle of the 14th century, the Te Arawa tribe settled here, living peacefully, until conflicts broke out among them causing a cleft in this tribe. With the arrival of other Maori tribes, the area soon became one of unrest and conflict. Upon the arrival of the Europeans in Rotorua in 1838, a missionary base was founded. In 1870, the tourist industry had already taken root due to the therapeutic effect of the hot springs. Thus, this city gained renowned as a health resort for those with rheumatism.

Rotorua / **Sights**

The main attraction of this region are the geothermal areas and the outdoor museum of →*Whakarewarewa.* However, this city has quite a lot to offer as well. It is situated on the beautiful *Lake Rotorua, (→Lakes)* and it also makes an interesting city to stroll through. In the centre of Rotorua is a beautiful park, *Government Gardens,* where one can catch a glimpse of *Tudor Towers,* which formerly housed the therapeutic baths. Today, this building houses the first class restaurant, the *Rotorua Museum,* and the *Art Gallery.* Those who do not want to miss a relaxing swim in the hot springs pools will find the opportunity in Government Gardens: on Hinemoa Street are the *Polynesian Pools,* filled with the water from the hot springs. In addition, many hotels and private homes have their own hot springs in the gardens.

After an impressive stroll along the beach, one will come upon the Maori village of *Ohinemutu.* The residents of this village welcome visitors, and one can imagine what it was like during the times of the European settlement. Saint Faith's Church, built in 1910, is also worth seeing especially because it is embellished with Maori art.

Five kilometres (3 miles) outside of Rotorua heading toward →*Hamilton,* one will find the *Rainbow & Fairy Springs,* a farm which breeds sheep and trout.

Here, one can gain an impression of life on a sheep and trout farm from 8 am to 5 pm. Admission costs NZ$ 12. Situated 3 kilometres (2 miles) away is the *Agrodome*. This is a tourist area where one can learn just about everything there is to know about sheep.

A number of tours are offered to the beautiful areas surrounding Rotorua.

Rotorua / **Museums and Galleries**

The *Museum in Tudor Towers* offers an interesting cross-section of representative pieces of Maori art, information on the eruption of the Tarawera volcanoes and a detailed presentation of the development of the Rotorua region, concentrating on geology and vegetation. The museum is open weekdays from 10 am to 4 pm and during weekends from 1 to 4:30 pm.

in the same building, one can visit the *Art Gallery* which exhibits pieces by New Zealand artists. The gallery is open during the same hours as the museum.

Rotorua / **Practical Information**

Accommodation

One of the hotels in the luxury class is the *Sheraton,* corner of Fenton and Sala Street, Tel: (7) 348 71 39, singles and doubles NZ$ 214. The *Havana Motel,* 12 Whakaue Street, Tel: (7) 348 81 34, charges NZ$ 67 for singles and doubles. Since most of the motels are concentrated along Fenton Street, comparing prices will prove beneficial.

Guest houses can be found almost everywhere. Examples are the *Mount View Lodge,* Mount View Drive, Tel: (7) 346 19 08, singles NZ$ 30, doubles NZ$ 50, or the *Eaton Hall,* Hinemaru Street, Tel: (7) 347 03 66, singles NZ$ 35, doubles NZ$ 56.

The *Rotorua Youth Hostel,* corner of Eruera and Hinemaru Street, Tel: (7) 347 68 10, costs NZ$ 13.

A small selection of the numerous camping sites: two are located on Whittaker Road; the first is *Cozy Cottage,* Tel: (7) 837 93, tent sites from NZ$ 6.50, cottages from NZ$ 18 and the other is *Lakeside Motor Camp,* Tel: (7) 896 13, charging comparable prices. The *Rotorua Thermal Motor Camp,* is equipped with a swimming pool, Tel: (7) 883 85, costing NZ$ 8 per person.

Entertainment: Definitely recommended are the Maori concerts, but there is also the more familiar night life offered in *Tudor Towers* and *Club Keets,* Pukuatua Street. Some of the pubs in Rotorua also offer live music.

Medical Care: Queen Elizabeth Hospital, Whakaue At., Tel: (7) 348 11 99 or Rotorua Medical Centre, 9 Amohia St., Tel: (7) 447 00 00.

Restaurants: Quick, light meals can be found just about everywhere in Rotorua. Worth recommending is *Gazebo,* Tutanekai St. Greek and Italian cuisine can be found in *Floyd's Café,* 46 Haupapa Street. In addition, there are a number of pizzerias in Rotorua. One should definitely try "hangi," the typical Maori dish. This is made from just about everything edible — meat, fish and vegetables — wrapped in large leaves and put in a hole in the ground with hot rocks. The hangi is then covered with damp cloths and soil to cook. After a few hours it is removed and served — a delicious treat. The hotels Travelodge and THC offer "hangi" parties with a Maori show. The price is NZ$ 30.

Transportation: Rotorua has good buses and flights to other larger cities.

Important Addresses:

The *NZTP office* is located at 67 Fenton Street, open from 8:30 am to 7pm. Additional information is available from the *Department of Conservation,* Amohau Street, open Monday to Friday from 9 am to 5pm.

Police: Rotorua District Headquarters, Fenton Street, Tel: (7) 348 00 99.

Post Office: Located on the corner of Hinemoa Street and Tutanekai Mall.

Russell

A quiet, laid-back city, Russell's significance is due to its location on the →*Bay of Islands.* Earlier, it served as the "temporary" capital of New Zealand because it was the largest European settlement.

Russell / **Sights**

One of the oldest churches in New Zealand is in Russell, *Christ Church,* built in 1835. Another of the country's older buildings also stands in this city, the *Pompallier House,* built in 1831 for the French missionary Bishop Pompallier. A small museum is housed here, open daily from 10 am to 12:30 pm and from 1:30 to 4:30 pm, admission is NZ$ 3. The actual museum is the *Captain Cook Memorial Museum,* located in the direct vicinity of the Pompallier House. In addition to the many exhibitions pertaining to the history of the early settlement, a replica of Captain James Cook's ship "The Endeavour" is also on

---

Visitors enter the museum village of Whakarewarewa through the elaborately decorated gateway ▶

display. The museum is open daily from 10 am to 4 pm, admission NZ$ 2. Another building among New Zealand's oldest is also located in Russell: the *Duke of Marlborough Hotel* on the beach promenade which was the first hotel in the country to be granted a licence to serve alcoholic beverages.

Russell / **Practical Information**

Accommodation: In the *Duke of Marlborough,* Tel: (9) 403 78 29, singles and doubles cost NZ$ 65. *Motel Russell,* Matauwhi Bay Road, Tel: (9) 403 78 54, singles cost NZ$ 54 and doubles NZ$ 62.

Car Rental: The "Budget" office is located at 41 Shotover Street; "Hertz" and "Newmans," on Church Street.

Restaurants: The *Duke of Marlborough,* on the Beach Promenade, can be recommended as well as *Gables* located in the same area. In addition, there are a number of snack bars as well as pubs and cafés.

Important Addresses: At the end of the boat docks is the *Information Centre,* and offering comprehensive information on the Bay of Islands is the *Bay of Islands Park Headquarters,* next to the Cook Memorial Museum. It is open weekdays from 7:30 am to 4 pm.

Post Office: Located on the corner of York and Chapel Street.

Shantytown

About eight kilometres (5 miles) south of →*Greymouth,* is the fully restored gold rush city of Shantytown. It is similar to →*Arrowtown,* but maintains the atmosphere of the gold rush era. The beautiful houses from the turn of the century awaken a nostalgic feeling as one rides through the town in a horse-drawn carriage. In addition, it is also possible to travel into the bush in a train with a steam locomotive from the year 1897. One can also give prospecting a try. Shantytown can be visited daily from 9 am to 5 pm. Admission is NZ$ 4.

Shopping

Souvenirs of a trip to New Zealand or presents for those who stayed behind can be found everywhere — even in the smallest of towns, there will at least be a store with New Zealand knickknacks. Maori carvings from everyday objects to decorative objects are also widely available. In →*Auckland,* the selection is the largest, however, typical and more original pieces can be more easily found in the smaller cities. Jewellry stores seem to be just about everywhere;

jade is one of the best sellers. Jewellry made from blue-green shellfish can only be found along the western coast, but is also available in Auckland.

The flightless kiwi has become the symbol of New Zealand and can be found in just about every form in the souvenir shops.

Practical and relatively inexpensive souvenirs are the wool sweaters available. Another option is to buy the typical "Swanny," a plaid jacket made from a durable wool material, which is not missing from any New Zealander's wardrobe because of its practicality, its warmth and weatherproofing. Sheep skin products are also very popular.

Those cooking their own meals will find an ample number of grocery stores in New Zealand. The selection in the supermarkets is large, although the prices might be higher. One will have to become accustomed to the store hours: supermarkets close at 5 o'clock in the evening, but at least they are also open on Saturdays. For everyday needs, the "dairies" can be found on almost every corner. These are usually also open during the weekends. Milk, bread, butter, eggs, canned goods, newspapers and other items can be purchased here. All of this is somewhat more expensive, but for small shopping lists, this will prove the most convenient. In smaller towns, dairies also makes a popular meeting place for the local residents.

Sights

The beauty of nature is the main attraction of New Zealand. In a relatively small area are impressively diverse landscapes including volcanoes, fjords, geysers, geothermal springs, glaciers, extensive beaches, mountain ranges and pristine forests. Experiencing this diversity is best accomplished by hiking and touring through the total of twelve national parks (→*National Parks*).

Information on New Zealand's history as well as on the Polynesian culture, fauna, flora and the Maori culture can not only be found in →*Auckland,* →*Wellington,* →*Christchurch* and →*Rotorua,* but also in numerous other villages and towns. Maori culture comes to life in →*Whakarewarewa.* This town is clearly laid out for tourists, serving the function of an outdoor museum. There are also geysers, hot springs and mud pools which can be enjoyed in many areas of the North Island without the masses of tourists.

Sports

Above all, the New Zealanders love their sports. It is not surprising then that diverse recreational activities are offered.

A few classic examples of sports offered in New Zealand are: **fishing,** an especially popular sport in New Zealand. One can fish along almost the entire coast, in the rivers and in many of the lakes. **Deep-sea fishing** is especially enjoyable. Information can be obtained from the "Hunting and Fishing Officer," NZTP Travel Office, Private Bag, Rotorua. Fishing licences are available only in NZTP Offices, priced at about NZ$ 55. Fishing gear can quite often be rented, even at some of the smaller motor camps.

Mountain Climbing and **hiking** is possible in all of the national parks and tour guides can even be arranged if so desired. The NZTP offices will be able to assist by providing excellent information and important weather reports.

Canoeists will be able to find ample information from the "New Zealand Canoeing Association," P.O. Box 5125 Auckland, New Zealand.

Horseback riding is also a wonderful experience in New Zealand. Whether the excursion on horseback lasts for hours, a day or even several days, the selection of tours offered is diverse and offered in almost every town. Hilton Hoss Hire is near Geraldine, offers, for example hour or day-long excursions at a price of around NZ$ 11 per hour.

Sailing is an especially enjoyable in the →*Bay of Islands,* →*Marlborough Sounds* and →*Fjordland* as it is along many of the sections of coastline. "Rainbow Yacht Charters" is the most widely known company. For NZ$ 180 per day, one can enjoy this form of holiday activity. Information is available at the Opua Post Office, Bay of Islands, Tel: (885) 278 21.

Skiing is, of course, only possible during the winter months in New Zealand, and then the best conditions are on the South Island. Helicopter skiing and organised ski tours are also offered. A day lift ticket costs between NZ$ 28 and NZ$ 40; heli-skiing, approximately NZ$ 350 per day. Ski equipment can be rented in the various sporting goods stores in the ski areas. Information is available by contacting "Ski Guides Ltd.," P.O. Box 177, Wanaka, New Zealand, Tel: Wanaka 7-930.

With a fountain reaching a height of 98 feet, the Pohutu geyser in Whakarewarewa is the largest in New Zealand ▶

Surfing and wind surfing are increasing in popularity. The opportunities are countless. Information is available through the "New Zealand Surfriders Association," P.O. Box 737, New Plymouth, and at "New Zealand Boardsailing Association," P.O. Box 37213, Parnell, Auckland.

Information about **scuba diving** is available through the "New Zealand Underwater Association," AA Mutual Building, Auckland.

Stewart Island

The two main islands of New Zealand offers so much that it is often forgotten that there are a number of smaller islands that also form part of New Zealand. Stuart Island is separated from the South Island from the Foveaux Strait with an area of 1,680 square km (649 square miles).

The landscape is characterised by extensive forests. Only a few "tracks" lead through the jungle, making it possible to experience the diverse species of birds on Stuart Island. Not only will one be able to enjoy the birds, but one will also make the acquaintance of the annoying sandflies (→Animals and Wildlife).

When following the history of Stewart Island, a strong possibility exists that the Moa hunters lived here before the arrival of the Maori. Stuart Island was first "discovered" by Captain James Cook in 1770. At first he thought it a peninsula and, for this reason, called it Cape South.

It was William Stewart, first officer of the Pegasus, who determined that this was an island. In 1864, the New Zealand government purchased the island from the Maori, for a price of £6,000. The one town which can be found on Stewart Island is Oban, also known as Halfmoon Bay. This town has a population of about 450, who live mainly from the fishing industry, but increasingly from tourism. Tourists can reach Stewart Island by airplane from Invercargill or by ferry from the port in Bluff. Rather than a 20 minute flight from Invercargill, one must first travel by bus and then ferry, taking approximately three hours. Meanwhile, 20 kilometres (12½ miles) of roadways surround Oban. Otherwise hiking boots are imperative in exploring the beauty of this island. Information is available in Oban, although one can also inquire at the "Lands and Survey Department" in the Menzies Building across from the train station. The small settlement of Oban is home to a museum, a hotel with a pub and a golf course. There is a small campsite and accommodation is also available in private homes. Along the hiking trails, one will find small, simple cabins which were built to provide hikers with a place to spend the night.

Tasman Glacier

New Zealand is also the "land of the glacier." In total, one will find over 100 of these rivers of ice. Tasman Glacier is the largest, and, as is true of many of the other glaciers, originates in the altitudes of Mount Cook. Measuring 29 kilometres (18 miles) in length, this is the longest glacier outside of the polar regions. "Mount Cook Airlines" is one of several companies offering glacier tours. In a light aircraft, one can actually land on the glacier. Guided ski tours are also possible. Information is available from the Park Visitors Centre.

Taupo

Taupo is a quaint city in the heart of the North Island. It is of interest for those who enjoy water sports because of the Taupo Lake. Hot springs and numerous rivers flow into this, the largest lake in New Zealand. A broad range of sports attract the visitors: water-skiing, swimming and boating. Especially popular is fishing, as many different types of trout are found in this lake.

The regions surrounding Taupo have more to offer than the city itself.

Huka Falls: leaving Taupo on the State Highway 1 heading toward Wairakai and Rotorua, turn right at the first main road. One will soon reach a pedestrian bridge over the Waikato River which falls over the Huka Falls, plunging 25 metres (79 feet). Even though there are an abundance of waterfalls in New Zealand, a trip to Huka Falls is very much worthwhile. Nearby is *Huka Village,* a replica of a village from the era of the first pioneers. It can be visited from 9 am to 5 pm, admission is NZ$ 3.

On the Waikato River, the longest river in New Zealand with a length of 425 kilometres (268 miles), is the "Wairakei Geothermal Power Station." New Zealand was the second country in the world to gain energy from geothermal sources. The numerous turbines are driven by geysers. Tours begin at the "Geothermal Power Project Information Office." The power station is open from 9 am to noon and from 1 to 4:30 pm.

Other sights near Taupo are →*Craters of the Moon* and →*Orakei Korako.*

Taupo / **Practical Information**
Accommodation

Manuel's Beach Resort, Lake Terrace Tel: (7) 378 51 10, singles NZ$ 112, doubles NZ$ 146. *Bradshaw's Travel Hotel,* Heuheu St., Tel: (7) 378 82 88, singles NZ$ 356, doubles NZ$ 50. Motels range from NZ$ 70 to NZ$ 100.

Campsites are also abundant in Taupo: *Auto Park,* Rangatira St., Tel: (7) 378 42 72, tent sites NZ$ 6.50, cottages are also available. *Taupo Cabins,* 50 Tonga St., Tel: (7) 378 43 46, offers various cabins priced from NZ$ 22. *Hill Top Motor Caravan Park,* 39 Purivi St., Tel: (7) 378 52 47 costs NZ$ 8 for a tent site.

Medical Care: Taupo Hospital, Kotara St., Tel: (074) 88-100 or Taupo Medical Centre, 117 Heuheu St., Tel: (074) 84-080.

Restaurants: Restaurants which can be recommended but are not inexpensive are *Echo Cliff,* 5 Tongariro St., and *Brookes,* 22 Tuwharetoa St. The *Steak & Ale Bar,* 17 Tongariro St., is also good, offering a wide selection.

Important Addresses: The *Taupo Information Centre,* Tongariro Street, is open daily from 8:30 am to 5 pm.

Police: Taupo Police Station, Starey Place Tel: (7) 378 60 60.

Post Office: Corner of Horomatangi and Ruapehu Street.

Tauranga

The largest city on the →*Bay of Plenty,* Tauranga is also the provincial capital. Mount Maunganui is located near to Tauranga. Tauranga itself is very clearly laid out, spread over three peninsulas interconnected by bridges. The centre is located on the middle peninsula, on Tauranga Wharf.

Tauranga / **Sights**

One should also be sure to visit the *Historic Village* on 17th Avenue. Here, one can travel back to the time of the first settlers and witness first hand how they lived during that time. One will find remnants of the early Maori settlement as well as the gold rush era. Workshops are in operation and there is also an old steam locomotive. The historical outdoor museum is open from 10 am to 4 pm and admission is NZ$ 5. An old Maori canoe is also on display along the promenade.

On Mission Street, one will not only find the oldest gardens in New Zealand, but one of the oldest buildings, the *Mission House,* as well.

For relaxation, the *Fernland Natural Mineral Pools* are the right address. They are located on Waihi Road and are open daily from 10 am to 10 pm.

Tauranga is also a good base for boat excursions or deep-sea fishing.

The Kauri trees can grow to majestic dimensions ▶

Tauranga / **Practical Information**

Accommodation

Tauranga Motel, The Strand, Tel: (7) 578 70 79, singles NZ$ 71 doubles NZ$ 82. Located centrally is *Willow Park Hotel,* Willow St., Tel: (7) 578 91 19, singles NZ$ 99, doubles NZ$ 115 as well as the *Fauntain Court Motel,* Turret Road, Tel: (7) 578 94 01, singles NZ$ 54, doubles NZ$ 66.

The *Tauranga Youth Hostel,* Glasgow Street, charges NZ$ 11 per night.

Located near the centre of town is the *6th Avenue Tourist Court,* Tel: (7) 578 57 09. A tent site costs NZ$ 8.50, a cabin is priced from NZ$ 26. At the *Silver Birch Motor Park,* 101 Turret Road, Tel: (7) 578 46 03, tent sites are priced at NZ$ 8.50 and cabins from NZ$ 30.

Automobile Association: The office is located on the corner of Cameron Road and Hamilton Street.

Car Rental: "Avis," 81 Grey Street.

Entertainment: There is live music on Tuesdays and Saturdays in *Candyo's Nightclub,* 132 Devonport Road.

Medical Care: Tauranga Hospital, Cameron Road, Tel: (7) 577 88 00 or Tauranga Medical Centre, 51 Third Avenue, Tel: (7) 578 90 59.

Restaurants: *La Salle,* at the northern end of "The Strand" is good although relatively expensive. Other recommended restaurants are *Chez Panisse,* Devonport Road or the less expensive *Cook's Cove Restaurant,* The Strand. Also on Devonport Road are the *Devonport Café, Bryges Café* and *Le Café,* all serving lighter meals.

Important Addresses: Information is available at the Information Centre on The Strand, open weekdays from 9 am to 5 pm.

Police: Tauranga District Headquarters, Monmouth Street, Tel: (7) 578 81 99.

Post Office: On the corner of Grey and Spring Street.

Te Anau

This city is situated on Lake Te Anau and is known as "the gateway to Fjordland." Other than this, it is comprised mainly of souvenir shops and other tourist facilities that do not warrant a long visit. Excursions alone make Te Anau of interest: the *Glow-worm Caves, Milford Track* and hiking trails.

Te Anau / **Practical Information**

Accommodation

THC Te Anau Hotel, Te Anau Terrace, Tel: (3) 249 74 11, priced from NZ$ 200 per person. *Edgewater XL Motel,* 52 Te Anau Terrace, Tel: (3) 249 72 58, singles and doubles NZ$ 68. *Shakespeare House,* Dusky Street, Tel: (3) 249 73 49, singles NZ$ 59, doubles NZ$ 70.

The *Te Anau Youth Hostel,* Milford Road, Tel: (3) 249 78 47 charges NZ$ 11. *Te Anau Motor Camp,* Tel: (3) 249 74 57 is a spacious campsite with tent sites for NZ$ 6 per person, cabins from NZ$ 24. In the same price category is the *Mountain View Park,* Mokonui Road, Tel: (3) 249 74 62.

Medical Care: Fjordland Medical Practice, Bligh Street, Tel: (03) 2 497 007.

Restaurants: Those who enjoy eating steaks should try the *Southern Touch Steakhouse* on the outskirts of town toward Milford. Excellent fish is served in *Kepler's Restaurant,* Milford Road. Another restaurant is *Henry's Restaurant & Bar* in the THC Te Anau Hotel.

Important Addresses: Located in Te Anau is the *Fjordland National Park Visitors Centre,* Te Anau Terrace, open daily from 8 am to noon and from 1 to 5 pm.

Police: Police Station, 196 Milford Road, Tel: (3) 249 76 00.

Post Office: Town Centre Street.

Telephone

International calls can be placed from every public telephone. Local calls cost 20 cents and, from private homes, these are free of charge. Overseas calls cost around NZ$ 3.50 per minute.

Phone calls from private households are less expensive. In order to keep track of the charges, it is best to register the call as a "price required call." To do this, one must simply state the number from which one is placing the call. A while after the call is completed, the operator will call back with the price of the call. It is also possible to place calls at all of the post offices.

Thames

The small city of Thames is situated on the →*Coromandel Peninsula.* What is beautiful are the wooden houses, some former hotels and manor houses — reminders of the era when Thames was the largest city in New Zealand during the gold rush. This past is documented through the abandoned gold mine. The first European influence came through the construction of a missionary station in 1883. The battles with the Maori in the 1860's characterised the history of this city as well.

Thames / **Sights**

For those who would like more information on the gold rush era, the *Historical Museum* can be found on the corner of Cochrane and Pollens Street. It is open Monday to Saturday from 10 am to 4 pm, Sundays from 1 to 4 pm. The *Mineralogical Museum,* corner of Cochrane and Brown Street, is open Monday to Friday from 2 to 4 pm and Sundays from 10 am to 4 pm.

Thames / **Practical Information**

Accommodation

Brian Boru, corner of Pollen and Richmond Street, Tel: 865 23, singles NZ$ 45, doubles NZ$ 66. Motels range from NZ$60 to NZ$ 70.

Three kilometres (2 miles) north of Thames is the *Dickson Park Motor Camp,* Tel: 873 08. with tent sites for NZ$ 7. The Coromandel Peninsula has a number of other campsites in this price class.

Automobile Association: Pollen Street.

Restaurants: There is a large selection of restaurants, snack bars and cafés along Pollen Street. One nicer restaurant is the *Regency Room* in the Hotel Imperial or one can try *Pizza Cabin* on the same street, serving good Italian and international cuisine. Another restaurant worth mentioning is *The Boulanger,* 523 Pollen Street.

Important Addresses: *Thames Information Centre,* in Poritt Park on Queens Street, is open daily from 10 am to 4 pm, offering information on the entire Coromandel Peninsula in addition to the city of Thames.

Post Office: Also located on Pollen Street.

Time of Day

New Zealand is 18 (New York) to 21 hours (Los Angeles) ahead of the continental United States and 13 hours ahead of the United Kingdom.

Tourist Information

The magic word for tourists is "NZTP." The offices of the "New Zealand Tourist and Publicity Department" can be found in all of the larger cities. Main offices are in Auckland, Rotorua, Wellington, Christchurch, Dunedin and Queenstown *(→individual entries)*. These offices offer a diversity of informational materials; maps for cities and various other attractions are usually free of charge. The NZTP employees are very friendly and well informed about current events, and are happy to give recommendations on an individual basis. They will also be helpful in booking accommodations or excursions.

In smaller cities and towns without an NZTP office, there will almost always be a friendly and helpful tourist office.

Travel Documents

A visa is not required for a stay of less than three months. One must have a passport, valid for the entire duration of the stay in New Zealand. The return ticket will also be checked.

National driving licences are valid in New Zealand; however, an international licence could save possible delays.

Owing to the fact that health insurance is not accepted on an international basis, it is recommended that one take out a supplemental travel health insurance policy for the duration of the trip *(→Medical Care)*.

Certification of vaccination is not necessary when taking a direct flight to New Zealand. Those who stop over in other countries which require vaccinations should check on the requirements for each of these individual countries.

If bringing a pet, one must be aware of the quarantine regulations when entering New Zealand and returning to one's home country.

Travel in New Zealand

By Car

In New Zealand is built well and clearly marked. For many tourists, it is unusual to drive on the left-hand side of the road sitting in the right-hand seat of the car. It will take a while before one becomes accustomed to this and stops signalling with the wipers instead of the turn signal. It is best to drive with great precaution, as any resident of Great Britain who has had the opposite problem will agree.

By Motorcycle

It is very pleasant to travel by motorcycle because of the well paved roads. Agencies renting out motorcycles are not as common as those with cars, however, it is still possible to find some. Per day, one should expect to pay between NZ$ 50 and NZ$ 60 plus 13 cents per kilometre travelled. When renting a motorcycle, it is important to remember that rain showers are frequent during the New Zealand summer.

By Train

The extensive and well developed rail network of approximately 2,690 miles (4,275 km) makes it possible for the visitor to reach almost all of the most significant destinations in New Zealand while enjoying the diversity of the landscape. The entire country can be toured with the "InterCity" rail company. Most routes are offered daily. A few examples of prices: Auckland — Rotorua NZ$ 32; Auckland — Wellington NZ$ 74; Picton — Nelson NZ$ 23; Picton — Christchurch NZ$ 44; Christchurch — Dunedin NZ$ 43; Christchurch — Queenstown NZ$ 72. The various InterCity trains (the Trans-Alpine Express, the Silver Fern or the Bay Express) are not only popular because of their furnishings (dining car, spacious seating areas etc.) but also because of the information given on the countryside as one travels through it. One can also arranged organised tours and overnight trips. For information and reservations, contact the main office in Auckland (9) 579 25 00 or in Wellington (4) 472 54 09.

By Bus

Various bus lines offer service in all of the major cities as well as to all of the major points of interest. Bus fares are about the same as the prices for the trains. Some examples: Picton — Christchurch NZ$ 46; Christchurch — Queenstown NZ$ 65. Organised bus tours are offered as well. Six trips, lasting from 3 to 28 days, include visits to major points of interest, accommodation and meals.

During the peak season, special fares are offered for rail and bus travel. "Mount Cook Landline" offers the "Kiwi Coach Pass" for unlimited travel on any routes for NZ$ 213 for seven days or NZ$ 525 for 25 days. The state-operated "InterCity" company combines bus and rail travel. Eight days of unlimited travel cost NZ$ 299; 22 days, NZ$ 479. As a rule, city buses and taxis operate around the clock.

By Air

The national airline "Air New Zealand" offers flights to 24 New Zealand cities. "Mount Cook Airlines" and "Ansett" are also popular. Air travel is made more attractive by the special airfares offered, of course with special conditions. A flight from Auckland to Wellington will, however, put a dent in one's travel budget, costing about NZ$ 195; from Christchurch to Queenstown, NZ$ 224. One can get lucky and find a special fare from Auckland to Wellington for as little as

NZ$ 74. There are also flight packs including any four domestic destinations for NZ$ 370. A number of airplane or helicopter tours are offered, presenting the most beautiful sides of New Zealand from a bird's-eye view. One especially popular tour is in the Mount Cook region on the South Island, including a landing on one of the glaciers. This tour costs around NZ$ 150.

By Ship

The Cook Strait, separating the North and South Islands, makes travel between the islands possible only by air or by ferry. The ferry operates four times daily from Picton to Wellington and then returning to Picton. During the peak season, reservations are recommended. For this 3½ hour trip, one will pay NZ$ 28; for a vehicle, between NZ$ 75 and NZ$ 130 depending on the length. This fare is often included in the price of many rental cars.

Hitchhiking

New Zealand is a hitchhiker's paradise. Even private cars with five passengers will stop if they see a thumb held out on the side of the road. New Zealanders are always ready to help: they will offer tips and even take small detours to show their guests their city. It is not uncommon to be invited for a visit if passing through again. Those who really take a New Zealander up on such an offer will be pleasantly surprised at how glad they are to have a visit. The only place where one must be prepared for a long wait when hitchhiking is the South Island which has less traffic.

Travelling to New Zealand

It is important to acquire flight information and book well in advance because the less expensive flights are often completely booked up to four months before the peak season (October to January) begins. Comparing the prices of different airlines is certainly worth the effort.

Those who have the time and interest, can choose the option of planning their own air route on the way to New Zealand. Flights from the United States over the Pacific make a stop on the Hawaiian or other South Pacific Islands (like Fiji or the Cook Islands) a viable option. The Asian route from Europe offers stop-overs in Singapore, Hong Kong, Tokyo and/or Australia.

Vegetation

"Native bush" is the general term for the fascinating types of flora found in New Zealand. The types of plant life that cover the islands range from tropical rain forest to arctic alpine woods. About 80% of all of the more highly developed plants are indigenous only to New Zealand; some related species can, however, be found in Australia, South America and Africa. For example, special emphasis should be given to the mammoth trees like the very diverse types of Kauri (→*Waipoua Kauri Forest*) and Rata. Yet another type of plant growing here is the Christmas tree — the Maori call it Pohutukawa. The sight of this well-shaped tree with its large red blossoms is quite impressive.

Waipoua Kauri Forest

The beautiful area of Waipoua Kauri Forest is located in the northeastern portion of the North Island in the Northland region (→*Regions*), between →*Dargaville* and Hokianga Harbour. It is worth noting because the beautiful Kauri forests are still in existence here. During the time of the first Maori settlers, New Zealand was virtually covered with this type of spruce. However, the profiteering Europeans deforested large regions making this tree rare. These trees are up to 1500 years old reaching a height of 30 to 50 metres (98 to 165 feet) a circumference of four metres (13 feet) and a circumference of 10 to 15 metres (33 to 50 feet). The largest tree in New Zealand is the "Tanemahuta" — the lord of the forest — which can be reached in five minutes from the parking area. From another parking area (both parking areas are well designated on the map which is available at the park headquarters), one can admire two special attractions in this forest: after a short walk, one will come to the *Four Sisters,* four Kauri trees nestled closely together. If continuing the walk for another 15 minutes, one will reach the "Te Matua Ngahere" — "The father of the forest," the second largest tree in New Zealand.

Waitangi

This small settlement on the →*Bay of Islands* is connected with the town of →*Paihia* by the Waitangi River Bridge. Waitangi has a special historical significance: on February 6, 1840 the "Treaty of Waitangi" was signed. The treaty placed New Zealand under the control of the British crown and was signed in the *Treaty House,* built by James Busby in 1832. To this day the Maori and "pakehas" (the European settlers) celebrate the signing of this treaty on February 6 in front of the colonial building. There are often also protests claiming exploitation of the Maori through this treaty. The Treaty House is now a museum, open daily from 9 am to 5 pm. Admission costs NZ$ 3.50.

Next to the museum is the impressive assembly house *Whare Runanga*. It was built in 1840 and embellished with carvings representing all of the Maori tribes. Normally such a meeting house will only have the carvings of a single tribe (→*Whakarewarewa*). Also interesting to see on the beach of Waitangi is an old war canoe that could hold about 150 warriors.

Waitomo

the small city of Waitomo lies 200 kilometres (125 miles) south of Auckland in *King Country*. Its significance stems from the natural wonders in its vicinity: the *Caves of Waitomo* and the *Glow-worm Grotto*. These caves were first introduced to the European settlers by the Maori in 1887.

Waitomo / **Sights**

The *Waitomo Caverns* are a network of three caves which can all be toured. Waitomo translates to "water flowing through a hole." The most frequently visited cave is that with the *Glow-worm Grotto*. In the *Cave Museum,* there is an informative presentation about the caves, the water system and the life cycle of the glow-worms. After the presentation, one is led into the cave to board a boat, pulled through the cave by a cable as the guide explains more about the cave and the glow-worms. As soon as one's eyes have adjusted to the darkness, one will see an incredible number of these insects, giving the cave the appearance of a glowing crystal. The tour leads deeper into the caves on foot. The price for this tour is presently NZ$ 9.50.

Another point of interest on the street leading to the caves is the *Ohaki Maori Village,* an old restored village. It can be visited daily from 10 am to 5 pm and costs NZ$ 3.50 admission.

Waitomo / **Practical Information**

Accommodation: The *THC Waitomo Hotel,* Tel: 882 27, costs NZ$ 101 for singles and doubles. Its advantage is that it is located close to the caverns. Other possibilities are the *Hangatiki Motel,* Tel: 882, priced from NZ$ 60 or the *Waitomo Country Lodge,* Tel: 81 09, doubles NZ$ 75, singles NZ$ 65. The *Waitomo Caves Camp & Caravan Park,* Tel: 876 39, has tent sites for NZ$ 6 or rooms from NZ$ 18 for two persons. Reservations can also be made here for cavern tours.

Restaurants: The only restaurant is in the *THC Waitomo Hotel.* This restaurant is, however, relatively expensive. There are also relatively expensive snacks available in the Cave Museum.

Wanaka

The town of Wanaka lies approximately 100 kilometres (63 miles) from →*Queenstown* directly on the shores of Lake Wanaka *(→Lakes),* which has fostered the development of this town into a tourist centre. Tourists from all over the world make the city a lively place during the entire year. In addition to the lake, Wanaka is a good starting point for an excursion to *Mount Aspiring National Park (→National Parks).*

Wanaka / **Practical Information**

Accommodation: Since Wanaka is predominantly a tourist centre, there is a large selection of accommodation. Located centrally on Hellwick Street is the *THC Wanaka Hotel,* Tel: (3) 43 78 26, doubles and singles from NZ$ 73; or the *Wunderview Motel* on Brownston Street, Tel: (3) 443 74 80, doubles NZ$ 56, singles NZ$ 51.

For campers: the *Penrith Park* on Beacon Point, Tel: (3) 70 09 for NZ$ 6 per person or the *Wanaka Motor Park* on Brownston Street, Tel: (3) 78 83 for NZ$ 7.50. The *Pleasant Lodge Caravan Park* is located three kilometres (2 miles) outside of Wanaka on Glendhu Bay Road, Tel: (3) 73 60, charging NZ$ 6.50 per night.

Medical Care: Wanaka Surgery, 37 Russell Street, Tel: (3) 443 78 11.

Restaurants: Highly recommended is the restaurant *Ripples* at the Pembroke Mall. Somewhat less expensive but also good is *Te Kano Café* on Brownston Street. This café also offers vegetarian meals. Excellent Italian cuisine is available in the *Cappricio* on the mall, or try the restaurant *First Café* on Artmore Street.

Important Addresses: Information is available at either the *Mount Aspiring Park Headquarters* or the *Visitors Centre,* corner of Ballantyne and Main Road.
Police: Police Station, Hellwick Street, Tel: (3) 443 72 72.
Post Office: Artmore Street when heading toward Cromwell.

Wanganui

The city of Wanganui lies at the mouth of the longest navigable river in New Zealand at the Tasman Sea — the Wanganui River. Today, this city no longer hold the importance that it once did. Earlier, this city was the centre of trade and commerce for the entire region including Wellington.

Wanganui / **Sights**

The beauty of Wanganui, one of the oldest cities in New Zealand, is brought out through the numerous parks and gardens. Especially popular points of interest are the *Queens Park* in the centre of the city or the *Lady Virginia Park* on Great North Road toward Plymouth.

The *Wanganui Museum,* located in Queens Park offers visitors insight into the Maori culture. Located here are also *Sarjeant Gallery* and the public library. The museum is open weekdays from 9:30 to 4:30 pm, weekends from 1 to 5 pm. Admission costs NZ$ 2. The gallery is open weekdays from 10:30 am to 4pm, Saturdays from 10:30 am to noon and Sundays from 1:30 to 4 pm. At the end of Victoria Avenue, one will cross the Wanganui River. Directly to the left of the bridge is the wooden carved gateway to *Durie Hill.* After going through the pedestrian tunnel, the ride in the lift to the top as well as the observation tower offer a beautiful of the city and countryside all the way to Mount Egmont and Mount Ruapehu in Tongariro National Park. This trip costs only 40 cents. The lift is in operation from Monday to Friday 7:30 am to 7pm, Saturdays from 9 am to 8 pm and Sundays from 10 am to 4 pm. Continuing to the right of the bridge a few miles further is the *Putiki Church,* a meeting place for the Maori carvers.

Wanganui / **Practical Information**

Accommodation: *Alwyn Motor Court,* Karaka, Tel: (6) 345 45 00, singles and doubles NZ$ 52. *Burwood Manor,* Dublin Street, Tel. (6) 345 21 80, singles and doubles NZ$ 74. *Abel Tasman Motel,* Pukiti Dr., Tel: (6) 345 09 43, singles NZ$ 59, doubles NZ$ 72. Another nice accommodation is the *Riverside Inn,* 2 Plymouth St., Tel: (6) 325 29, singles NZ$ 33, doubles NZ$ 45. *Castle Cliff Camp,* Tel: (6) 345 56 99, tent sites for NZ$ 7 per person.

Automobile Association: The office is located at the corner of Victoria Avenue and Ridgeway Street.

Medical Care: Wanganui Base Hospital, Heads Road, Tel: (6) 345 39 09 or Wicksteed House, 220 Wicksteed St., Tel: (6) 345 82 99.

Restaurants: There are only two restaurants offering a small selection of dishes: *Joseph's,* at 13 Victoria Avenue and *Bistro 99 The Strand,* corner of Guyton and St. Hill Street. Sandwiches and fast food can be easily found.

Important Addresses: On Guyton Street between St. Hill and Wilson Street is the *Information Centre,* open weekdays from 8:30 am to 5 pm and weekends from 9 am to 2 pm.

Police: Police Headquarters, Bell Street, Tel: (6) 345 44 88.

Post Office: Ridgeway Street.

Wellington

Wellington is the impressive capital of New Zealand, known to the populace as "Windy Wellington." Since Wellington lies on the southern tip of the North Island, a brisk breeze blows here during the entire year. The city has a population of 321,000. Wellington has a lot to offer in the way of entertainment, making it possible to become acquainted with the modern New Zealand lifestyle. Wellington is situated in a landscape of bays and rolling green hills.

Wellington / **History**

The Maori legends recount that the navigator Kupe was first to sail into the harbour of Wellington. Later, various Maori tribes settled here, living in harmony with nature until selling this land to Wakefield, the founder of the "New Zealand Company." Consequently, Wellington was to become the first settlement developed by this company in 1840.

A few settlers made this settlement their new home; at first, it was no easy task to develop the necessary infrastructure. On the one hand, Wellington was to be developed for commercial trade due to its harbour, and plans were already being made for the surrounding areas. Complicating this was the fact that the Maori felt swindled in the sale of this land. Conflicts resulted.

Eventually, the settlement slowly expanded around the harbour and Lambton Quay area. A number of houses were then built on the surrounding hills. During the gold rush, the South Island increased in significance — the reason for moving the governmental seat from Auckland to Wellington in 1840. This port became the most important because of its close proximity to the South Island. For this reason, Wellington gained even more importance as a traffic transport and communication despite the two earthquakes in 1848 and 1855

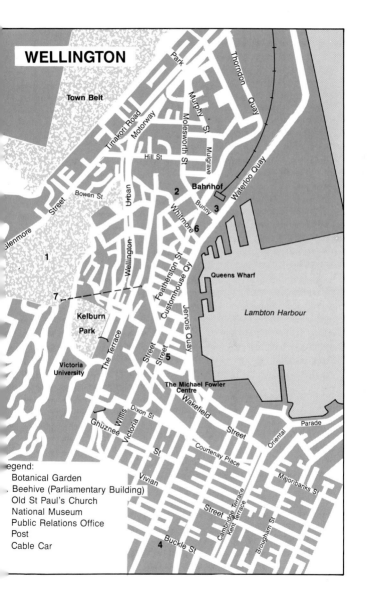

WELLINGTON

Town Belt

Park

Thorndon Quay

Motorway

Tinakori Road

Murphy St.

Molesworth St.

Mulgrave

Hill St

Waterloo Quay

Bowen St

Urban

2

Bahnhof

Bunny

3

Whitmore

6

Glenmore

Street

Wellington

1

Featherston St

Customhouse Qy

Jervois Quay

Queens Wharf

Lambton Harbour

7

Kelburn Park

The Terrace

Street

Street

5

Victoria University

The Michael Fowler Centre

Wakefield

Dixon St

Ghuznee

Willis

Victoria

St

Street

Oriental

Parade

Courtenay Place

Vivian

Street

Cambridge Terrace

Kent Terrace

Majoribanks St

Brougham St

4

Buckle St

Legend:
1. Botanical Garden
2. Beehive (Parliamentary Building)
3. Old St Paul's Church
4. National Museum
5. Public Relations Office
6. Post
7. Cable Car

Wellington / **Sights**

In order to gain an overview of this spread out city, it is best to take a ride on one of the famous *cable cars*. On the main street of Wellington, Lambton Quay, there is a small side-street that leads to the terminal station of this attraction. These first began operation in 1902. The end station is in the district of Kelburn, and from Kelburn Hill, there is a wonderful view of the city and harbour.

On the way back down to the city, one should not pass up the chance to take a walk through the *Botanical Garden.* Also worth visiting is the Pavillon Café with its inviting violin music. The last part of this walk leads through a large, old cemetery. Then, one will cross the motorway on a pedestrian bridge leading back to the centre of town. On a stroll through the city, especially on Lambton Quay, the contrast between old and new is quite impressive.

The contrast of old and new is also apparent during a visit to the governmental district on Glenmore Street. The former *Government Building,* built entirely of wood and is the second largest wooden building in the world, is right next to the new Parliament Building, the *Beehive.* Tours of this building can be taken weekdays and information: Tel: 7949-199.

Not far from here, on Mulgrave Street, one should visit *Old Saint Paul's Church.* Although the church was first completed in 1864. The interior is characterised by the precision of the Gothic architectural style. It is open Monday to Saturday from 10 am to 4 pm and Sundays from 1 to 4 pm. Another attraction is the *Wellington Zoo,* located four kilometres (2¹/₂ miles) outside the city. The zoo is open daily from 8:30 am to 5 pm and admission costs NZ$ 4.

Wellington / **Museums and Galleries**

In the *National Museum* on Buckle Street, adjacent to the *National Art Gallery,* there are a number of interesting exhibits on the Polynesian and Maori cultures as well as the colonial period. Admission to the museum and gallery is free of charge and both are open daily from 10 am to 4:45 pm.

Wellington / **Practical Information**
Accommodation

James Cook Hotel, located on The Terrace, Tel: (4) 472 58 65, singles and doubles from NZ$ 236. *Saint George Hotel* on the corner of Willis and Boulcott, Tel: (4) 473 91 39, singles NZ$ 63 and doubles NZ$ 78. *Trekkers Hotel,* Upper Cuba Street, Tel: (4) 485 21 53, singles NZ$ 60, doubles NZ$ 70.

On The Terrace Street, one will find a number of guest houses, for example: *Victoria House Inc.* (Student Hotel), Tel: (4) 484 33 57, singles NZ$ 40, doubles NZ$ 68. *Ambassador Travel Lodge,* Tel: (4) 485 72 15, singles NZ$ 45, doubles NZ$ 52. *Terrace Travel Hotel,* Tel: (4) 482 95 06, singles NZ$ 51, doubles NZ$ 62. The *Wellington Youth Hostel,* 40 Tinakori Road, Tel: (4) 473 22 71, costs NZ$ 13 per night. Another hostel in Wellington is the *Beethoven House,* 89 Brougham St., Tel: (4) 484 22 26. Such accommodation is rare: Beethoven's music is played the entire day, smoking is prohibited, and it has a very special atmosphere with numerous festivities for only NZ$ 12 per night.

Wellington has very few camping sites. Fourteen kilometres (9 miles) outside of Wellington in Lower Hutt is the *Hutt Park Motor Camp,* Tel: (4) 568 59 13, with tent sites from NZ$ 7 per person.

Automobile Association: The office is located on Lambton Quay.

Car Rental: "Avis," as well as other car rental agencies, can be found at the airport. An Avis branch office is also located at 25 Dixon Street.

Entertainment: Although the night life in Wellington often appears subdued, in many of the downtown pubs, there is live music. There are a number of larger and smaller theatres like the *Wellington Repertory Theatre,* Dixon St., the *Downstage Theatre,* Cambridge Terrace and the *University Memorial Theatre.*

Medical Care: Wellington Hospital, Riddiford St., Newton, Tel: (4) 485 59 99 or Dr. Ernst Philipp, 99 The Terrace, Tel: (4) 473 75 71.

Restaurants: For Mexican food, the small *Mexican Cantina* is highly recommended, located at 19 Edward Street. One should be prepared to wait for a table. For Italian cuisine, try *La Spaghettata,* located at 15 Edward Street — good and inexpensive. For Indian food, the *Bengal Tiger,* at 33 Willis Street, is quite popular. There are also a number of Chinese restaurants like *The Horn Kung,* on Courtenay Place. Those who would prefer a steak can visit *Chloe's* in the Victualling Company Building built in 1860, at 152-172 Lambton Quay. For those who enjoy vegetarian cuisine: *That's Natural,* 88 Manners Mall.

Transportation: Wellington is a transportation hub on Cook Strait. Large and small airlines connect the larger cities in New Zealand. The bus also departs frequently. Connecting to the South Island are a number of flights or the ferry to Picton (→*Travel in New Zealand*).

Important Addresses: On Mercer Street is the *NZTP Office,* open Monday to Thursday from 8:30 am to 5 pm, Friday from 8:30 am to 8 pm and Saturday from 9:30 am to 12:30 pm. The *Public Relations Office* is also located on Mercer Street and is open daily from 9 am to 5 pm.

Police: Central Police Station, Johnston Street, Tel: (4) 472 30 00.

Post Office: Customhouse Quay.

Whakarewarewa

Whakarewarewa is the largest and most famous geothermal region in New Zealand and it is also a museum village located in the direct vicinity of →*Rotorua*. Visitors are greeted in Whaka (the shortened form of the village's name) by "Naumai Haere mai" — "Welcome to our world."

On a guided tour, one can learn about the buildings, their function and the original lifestyle. The most ritualistically important place is called "marae." No one may enter without asking permission or being invited to do so. The largest house is the assembly hall, embellished with wood carvings. The construction is in the symbolic form of a body: the main ceiling support is considered the spine, the braces are the ribs etc. The carvings in the meeting house refer only to one individual tribe; each individual carving represents an ancestor. Often the carvings appear to be grimacing, which can be explained in that the ancestors are considered sacred and one is not allowed to make exact images of them. The carvings symbolise the spiritual resting place of the ancestor and are not depictions of their worldly bodies.

Inside the meeting house — wearing shoes inside would be an insult to the tribe — are woven pictures called "tukatuka." Each has its own story to tell and are all directly related to the history of the tribe and the individual ancestors. A little farther along at the "marae" is the "food house," built on stilts. This storage building was not only used for food, but for all of the essentials of daily life called "tapu," meaning holy or sacred.

Directly behind the "marae" of Whaka is the geothermal region with bubbling mudpools as well as *Pohutu,* the largest geyser in New Zealand. The fountain shoots as high as 30 metres (98 feet) and the eruption is always "announced" by its smaller neighbour *Prince of Wales Feather.*

After a walking tour through the geothermal region, one will come upon the actual Maori village, still inhabited today. In some of the houses are souvenir shops where everything from knickknacks to authentic Maori carvings. The Hi-Tiki is the main symbol used in these carvings. This is also an ancestor known as the god of fertility.

Those who visit Whaka should not miss the Maori concert including the Haka, the war dance — often pictured on postcards — which ends with the dancers sticking out their tongues, a sign of aggression and warfare. The men wear the traditional "kete" or flax skirts and the women wear the "pare." The "mako" can also be seen here: these are the traditional tattoos. The chiefs, high priests and warriors often had their entire faces covered with spiral decorations. Even women with higher status in the tribe wore these tattoos on their chins.

From the narration that accompanies the Maori concert, one will learn that only the men were allowed to produce the wooden carvings. Only they were considered materialised spiritual beings or "tapu." (The only carving school in New Zealand is located in Whaka in the "Arts and Crafts Centre of Rotorua.") Women, created from the earth, are only allowed to lead tours for visitors. Admission is NZ$ 15 including the Maori concert.

Whangarei

Whangarei is the most important city in the Northland region (→*Regions)* and is renowned for Whangarei Harbour. This city, with its population of 45,000, is also home to New Zealand's only oil refinery.

Whangarei / **Sights**

The main attraction here is the *Chapham Clock Museum* in the *Central Park Rose Gardens.* Eight hundred watches and clocks are exhibited here in every shape and size. The oldest piece dates back to 1636. The museum is open daily from 10 am to 4 pm, admission is NZ$ 2.50.

Another attraction are the *Whangarei Falls,* about 6 kilometres (4 miles) outside the city on the Ngunguru Road.

Whangarei / **Practical Information**

Accommodation: *Grand Establishment,* corner of Rose and Bank Street, Tel: (9) 438 42 79, singles NZ$ 54, doubles NZ$ 69. Motels are also abundant, although rather expensive: *Ascot Motel,* 7 Matipo Place, Tel: (9) 438 15 99, singles NZ$ 56, doubles NZ$ 68. *Kamo Motel,* 352 Kamo Rd., Tel: (9) 435 10 49, singles NZ$ 59, doubles NZ$ 70. *Cherry Court Motor Lodge,* 35 Otaika Rd., Tel: (9) 438 31 28, singles NZ$ 77, doubles NZ$ 84. Guest houses include: *Kingswood Manor,* 260 Kamo Rd., Tel: (9) 437 57 79. Prices start at NZ$ 70 including breakfast. The *Whangarei Youth Hostel,* 52 Punga Grove Avenue, Tel: (9) 438 89 54, costs NZ$ 11 per night.

Very close to the centre of town is the *Alpha Caravan Park,* 34 Tarewa Rd., Tel: (9) 438 98 76. A tent site costs NZ$ 7 per person; a cottage starts at NZ$ 35 for two people. In the same price class is the *Otaika Caravan Park,* 136 Otaika Rd., Tel: (9) 438 14 59. About three kilometres outside the city is the *William Jones Camp,* Mair St., Tel: (9) 438 78 46, a tent site costs NZ$ 5.

Automobile Association: The office is on the corner of The Mall and Bank St.

Medical Care: Northland Base Hospital, Hospital Road, Tel: (9) 438 20 79 or Rust Avenue Medical Centre, 15 Rust Ave., Tel: (9) 438 41 81.

Restaurants: Restaurants include the *Quo Vadi,* 24 Water St. and *Forum Restaurant* on Calfer Avenue in the "Forum North Civic Centre." In addition, *Plumes Restaurant* can also be recommended, located at 63 Bank Street as can *Timothy's Mythe,* 58 Vine Street.

Important Addresses: The *Information Office* is located on Calfer Ave., in the Forum North Civic Centre.

Police: Whangarei Police Station, Lower Cameron Street, Tel: (9) 438 73 39.

Post Office: Corner of Rathbone and Robert Street.